Indian Ink

A play

Tom Stoppard

A SAMUEL FRENCH ACTING EDITION

SAMUEL FRENCH

FOUNDED 1830

SAMUELFRENCH.COM
SAMUELFRENCH-LONDON.CO.UK

FOR PRODUCTION ENQUIRIES

UNITED STATES AND CANADA
Info@SamuelFrench.com
1-866-598-8449

UNITED KINGDOM AND EUROPE
Plays@SamuelFrench-London.co.uk
020-7255-4302

Each title is subject to availability from Samuel French, depending upon country of performance. Please be aware that *INDIAN INK* may not be licensed by Samuel French in your territory. Professional and amateur producers should contact the nearest Samuel French office or licensing partner to verify availability.

MUSIC USE NOTE

Licensees are solely responsible for obtaining formal written permission from copyright owners to use copyrighted music in the performance of this play and are strongly cautioned to do so. If no such permission is obtained by the licensee, then the licensee must use only original music that the licensee owns and controls. Licensees are solely responsible and liable for all music clearances and shall indemnify the copyright owners of the play(s) and their licensing agent, Samuel French, against any costs, expenses, losses and liabilities arising from the use of music by licensees. Please contact the appropriate music licensing authority in your territory for the rights to any incidental music.

IMPORTANT BILLING AND CREDIT REQUIREMENTS

If you have obtained performance rights to this title, please refer to your licensing agreement for important billing and credit requirements.

INDIAN INK

First produced by Michael Codron at the Yvonne Arnaud
Theatre, Guildford, and subsequently at the Aldwych
Theatre, London, on 27th February 1995 with the follow-
ing cast of characters:

Flora Crewe	Felicity Kendal
Coomaraswami	Rashid Karapiet
Nazrul	Ravi Aujila
Eleanor Swan	Margaret Tyzack
Eldon Pike	Colin Stinton
Questioner	Akbar Kurtha
Nirad Das	Art Malik
Anish Das	Paul Bhattacharjee
David Durance	Dominic Jephcott
Dilip	Akbar Kurtha
Englishman	Kenneth Jay
Englishwoman	Diana Oxford
Resident	Peter Wickham
Club Servant	Ravi Aujila
Rajah/Politician	Madhav Sharma
Rajah's Servant	Naim Khan-Turk
Nell	Nickie Rainsford
Eric	Daniel Wellon

Directed by Peter Wood
Designed by Carl Toms
Lighting by Mark Henderson

CHARACTERS

Flora Crewe
Coomaraswami
Nazrul
Eleanor Swan
Eldon Pike
Anish Das
Nirad Das
David Durance
Dilip
Resident
Englishwoman
Englishman
Rajah/Politician
Nell
Eric

In addition:
Indian Questioner(s)
Club Servant(s)
Rajah's Servant(s)

The play is set in two periods, 1930 (in India) and mid-1980s (in England and India)

AUTHOR'S NOTE

It is not intended that the stage be demarcated between India and England, or past and present. Floor space, and even furniture, may be common. In this respect and in others, the play profited greatly from Peter Wood's direction. The stage directions generally follow the original production but are not offered as a blueprint for the staging.

T.S.

Indian Ink is dedicated to the memory of
Laura Kendal

Other plays by Tom Stoppard published by Samuel French Ltd

Albert's Bridge
Arcadia
Artist Descending a Staircase
Dirty Linen *and* New-Found-Land
The Fifteen Minute Hamlet
Hapgood
If You're Glad I'll Be Frank
Night and Day
The Real Inspector Hound
The Real Thing
Rosencrantz and Guildenstern Are Dead
A Separate Peace

with Clive Exton
The Boundary

ACT I

Dusk

Flora sits alone on a moving train. Her suitcase is on the rack above her head. The train is approaching a station. Flora, already speaking, stands to lift down her suitcase. By the end of her first speech, she is on the station platform at Jummapur

Flora "Jummapur, Wednesday, April the second. Darling Nell, I arrived here on Saturday from Bombay after a day and a night and a day in a Ladies Only, stopping now and again to be revictualled through the window with pots of tea and proper meals on matinée trays, which, remarkably, you hand back through the window at the next station down the line where they do the washing up; and from the last stop I had the compartment to myself, with the lights coming on for me to make my entrance on the platform at Jummapur. The President of the Theosophical Society was waiting with several members of the committee drawn up at a respectful distance, not quite a red carpet and brass band but garlands of marigolds at the ready, and I thought there must be somebody important on the train ——"

Coomaraswami (*interrupting*) Miss Crewe!

Flora "—— and it turned out to be me."

Coomaraswami Welcome to Jummapur!

Flora "—which was very agreeable." Thank you!

And as she is garlanded by Coomaraswami

How nice! Are you Mr Coomar ...

Coomaraswami Coomaraswami! That is me! Is this your only luggage?! Leave it there!

He claps his hands imperiously for assistance, and then shakes hands enthusiastically with Flora

How do you do, Miss Crewe!

The handshake which begins on the station platform ends on the verandah of the "Dak Bungalow", or guesthouse. The guesthouse requires a verandah and an interior which includes, or comprises, a bedroom. On the verandah is a small table with at least two chairs. There is an electric light, unlit, and an oil lamp, lit. The bedroom contains a bed under a mosquito net, a washstand, a bedside table, an electric fan and a "punkah". There is a door to a bathroom off stage

A servant, Nazrul, carries Flora's suitcase into the bedroom, and then retreats to his quarters, out of sight

Flora (*completing the handshake*) Thank you!
Coomaraswami Welcome, my dear Miss Crewe! And farewell! A day of rest!
Flora Thank you — you were so kind to ——
Coomaraswami I will leave you! Tomorrow, a picnic! Do you like temples?
Flora Well, I don't know ... I'm sure I ...
Coomaraswami Leave everything to me!

Coomaraswami leaves her, shouting in Hindi for his buggy-driver

The Shepperton garden is now visible. Here, Mrs Swan and Pike are having tea while occupied with a shoebox of Flora's letters

Flora "And in no time at all I was installed in a little house, two good-sized rooms under a tin roof... with electric light ..."

She tries the electric light switch without result

"... and an oil lamp just in case ..."

She looks out from the verandah

"... a verandah looking out at a rather hopeless garden ... but with a good table and chair which does very well for working ..."

She tries out the chair and the table

"... and a wicker sofa of sorts for not working ... and round the back ..."

She disappears around the corner of the verandah where it goes out of sight

Mrs Swan turns a page of the letter

Mrs Swan I wish I'd kept the envelopes, they'd be worth something now, surely, the Indian ones at least.

Pike Oh, but it's the wine, not the bottles! These letters are a treasure. They may be the only *family* letters anywhere.
Mrs Swan I dare say, since I'm the only family.
Pike Her handwriting sometimes ... (*He passes a letter to her for assistance*)
Mrs Swan (*deciphering where he indicates*) "... a kitchen bit with a refrigerator ..."

Flora reappears

Flora "... a kitchen bit with a refrigerator! But Nazrul, my cook and bottle-washer, disdains the electric stove and makes his own arrangements on a little verandah of his own."

She goes into the interior, into the bedroom, where she tries the switch for the electric fan, again without result

"My bedroom, apart from the electric fan, also has a punkah which is like a pelmet worked by a punkah-wallah who sits outside and flaps the thing by a system of ropes and pulleys, or would if he were here, which he isn't. And then off the bedroom ..."

She disappears briefly through a door

Mrs Swan passes the page to Pike and they continue to read in silence

Flora reappears

"... is a dressing-room and bathroom combined, with a tin tub, and a shower with a head as big as a sunflower — a rainflower, of course ..."

Pike grunts approvingly

"... and all this is under a big green tree with monkeys and parrots in the branches, and it's called a duck bungalow ..."
Mrs Swan *Dak* bungalow.
Flora "... although there is not a duck to be seen."

She disappears into the bathroom with her suitcase

Mrs Swan Dak was the post; they were post-houses, when letters went by runner.
Pike Ah ...
Mrs Swan I like to have two kinds of cake on the go. The Madeira is my own.

Pike I'm really not hungry.

Mrs Swan I wouldn't let that stop you, Mr Pike, if you hope to get on my good side.

Pike I would love some. The Madeira.

She cuts him a slice

And won't you please call me Eldon? (*He takes the slice of cake*) Thank you. (*He takes the bite and gives a considered verdict*) Wonderful.

Mrs Swan I should think so.

Pike It's the excitement. There's nothing like these in the British Library, you know!

Mrs Swan (*amused*) The British Library!

Pike The University of Texas has Flora Crewe indexed across twenty-two separate collections! And I still have the Bibliothèque Nationale next week. The "Collected Letters" are going to be a year of my life!

Mrs Swan A whole year just to collect them?

Pike (*gaily*) The notes, the notes! The notes is where the fun is! You can't just *collect* Flora Crewe's letters into a book and call it "The Collected Letters of Flora Crewe". The correspondence of well-known writers was mostly written without a thought for the general reader. I mean, they didn't do their own footnotes. So there's an opportunity here. Which you might call a sacred trust. Edited by E. Cooper Pike. There isn't a page which doesn't need — look — you see here? — "I had a funny dream last night about the Queen's Elm." Which Queen? What elm? Why was she dreaming about a *tree*? So this is where I come in, wearing my editor's hat. To lighten the darkness.

Mrs Swan It's a pub in the Fulham Road.

Pike Thank you. This is why God made poets and novelists, so the rest of us can get published. Would that be a *chocolate* cake?

Mrs Swan Why, would you ... ?

Pike No, I just thought: did your sister like chocolate cake particularly?

Mrs Swan What an odd thing to think. Flora didn't like chocolate in any form.

Pike Ah. That's interesting. May I? (*He takes the next page of the letter from the tea-table*)

Flora approaches, accompanied by Coomaraswami, who has a yellow parasol

Flora "The sightseeing with picnic was something of a Progress with the president of the Theosophical Society holding a yellow parasol over me while the committee bicycled alongside, sometimes two to a bike, and children ran before and behind — I felt like a carnival float representing Empire — or, depending how you look at it, the Subjugation of the Indian People, and of course you're right, darling, but I never saw anyone less subjugated than Mr Coomaraswami."

Coomaraswami We have better temples in the south. I am from the south. You are right to be discriminating!

Flora (*apologetically*) Did I seem discriminating? I'm sure it wasn't their fault. The insides of churches ...

Coomaraswami I understand you completely, Miss Crewe!

Flora But I don't know what I'm trying to say!

Coomaraswami That is not a requirement.

Flora I'm afraid I'm without religion, you see.

Coomaraswami I *do* see! Which religion are you afraid you are most without?

Flora Now, Mr Coomaraswami, turning a phrase may do for Bloomsbury but I expect better from *you*.

"And I told him about Herbert's lady decorator being asked on her deathbed what was her religion and telling the priest, 'I'm afraid I worship mauve'."

Coomaraswami (*thoughtfully*) For me, it is grey.

Flora "I'm going to like India."

Pike (*with letter*) Who was Herbert?

Mrs Swan Wells.

Pike Ah. (*Catching on*) H. G. Wells? Really? (*Cautiously*) You don't mean he and Flora ... ?

Mrs Swan You should see your face. Flora met him not long before she went out.

Pike Out?

Mrs Swan To India. It must have been round Christmas or New Year. I think I got a postcard from Paris (*She delves into the shoebox*) Flora loved Paris. Here, look ... is that it?

Pike Paris, yes ... no, 1924 ... it's a souvenir of the Olympic Games.

Mrs Swan Oh yes, the hurdler. Flora apologized publicly in the Chelsea Arts Club. No medals for us in the *hurdles*.

Pike Is that *true*, Eleanor?

Mrs Swan Now, Eldon, you are *not* allowed to write a book, not if you were to eat the entire cake. The *Collected Poems* was a lovely surprise and I'm sure the *Collected Letters* will be splendid, but *biography*, is the worst possible excuse for getting people wrong.

Flora "So far, India likes me. My lecture drew a packed house, Mr C's house, in fact, and a much more sensible house than mine, built round a courtyard with a flat roof all round so I had an audience in the gods like gods in the audience ..."

There is the sound of the applause. Coomaraswami faces the audience with
Flora. It is night. There may be a microphone for the public statements

"... and it all went terribly well, until ..."

Coomaraswami Miss Crewe in her wisdom and beauty has agreed to answer questions!

Flora "— and the very first one went ——"

Questioner Miss Crewe, it is said you are an intimate friend of Mr H. G. Wells ——

Flora "— and I thought, 'God, how unfair! — to have come all this way to be gossiped about as if one were still in the Queen's Elm' ——"

Pike A public house in the Fulham area of Chelsea.

Flora "— but it turned out nothing was meant by it except ——"

Questioner Does Mr Wells write his famous books with a typewriter or with pen and ink?

Flora (*firmly*) With pen and ink, a Waterman fountain pen, a present from his wife.

There is an appreciative hubbub

"Not that I had the least idea — Herbert showed small inclination to write his famous books while I was around."

Pike FC had met Wells no earlier than December and the affair was therefore brief, possibly the weekend of January 7th and 8th; which she spent in Paris.

Flora "After which there was a reception with lemonade and Indian Scotch ..."

Flora and Coomaraswami are offered drinks from a tray of drinks

They are joined in due course by the Questioner and then Das

"... and delicious snacks and conversation — darling, it's so moving, they read the *New Statesman* and the *TLS* as if they were the Bible in parts, well, I don't mean the Bible but you know what I mean, and they know who wrote what about whom; it's like children with their faces jammed to the railings of an unattainable park. They ask me ——"

Questioner What is your opinion of Gertrude Stein, Miss Crewe?

Flora Oh ... yes, Gertrude Stein! — "and I can't bring myself to say she's a poisonous old baggage who's travelling on a platform ticket ..."

Pike FC went to tea with Gertrude Stein and her companion Alice B. Toklas in Paris in 1922. The legend that Stein threw her out of the apartment because FC asked for the recipe of Miss Toklas's chocolate cake cannot be trusted. FC did not like chocolate in any form.

Flora "Then I met my painter ..."

Das Miss Crewe, may I congratulate you on your lecture. I found it most interesting!

Flora Thank you ...

Das I was surprised you did not mention Virginia Woolf.

Flora I seldom do.

Das Have you met George Bernard Shaw?

Flora Yes. I was nearly in one of his plays once.

Das But you are not an actress ... ?

Flora No, that was the trouble.

Das What do you think of Jummapur?

Flora Well, I only arrived the day before yesterday but ——

Das Of course. How absurd of me!

Flora Not at all. I was going to say that my first impression ——

Das Jummapur is not in any case to be compared with London. Do you live in Bloomsbury?

Flora No, I live in Chelsea.

Das Chelsea — of course! My favourite part of London!

Flora Oh! You ... ?

Das Yes, I hope to visit London one of these days. The Chelsea of Turner and the Pre-Raphaelite Brotherhood! — Rossetti lived in Cheen Walk! Holman Hunt lived in Old Church Street! *The Hireling Shepherd* was painted in Old Church Street! What an inspiration it would be to me to visit Chelsea!

Flora You are a painter!

Das Yes! Nirad Das.

Flora How do you do.

Das I am top hole. Thank you. May I give you a present?

Flora Oh ...

Das Please do not judge it too harshly, Miss Crewe ...

Flora Thank you!

Das Of course, I work in oils, Winsor and Newton. If it would please you to sit for your portrait I would like to repay you for your superfine portrait-in-words of the rough-and-tumble of literary life in London.

Flora Would you really?

Das I would very much!

Das produces a small sketch pad and tears off a sheet. He gives it to her shyly

Flora "... and he gave me a pencil sketch of myself holding forth on the literary life."

Flora retraces her steps with Coomaraswami. Das goes

Pike She mentions a pencil sketch. Do you know what happened to it?

Mrs Swan I'm sure I never saw it. I would have remembered if it had been among what was called her effects. It was only one suitcase.

Pike Do you still have it?

Mrs Swan What? Her suitcase? Heavens, it was a battered old thing even then, and being always on the move, Eric and I, one shed things ...

Pike You threw away Flora Crewe's suitcase?

Mrs Swan What is it you're up to, Eldon? A *luggage* museum? Really, you're like an old woman about her; except, of course, that I'm not.

Pike But she was Flora Crewe!

Mrs Swan (*crisply*) Well, if so, where was everybody sixty years ago?

Mrs Swan replenishes the teacups. Pike takes one or two more letters from the shoebox and scans them

At the guesthouse, Nirad Das arrives by bicycle. He has his wooden workbox strapped to the pillion-rack. His folded easel is strapped to his back. He rides one-handed. holding a canvas in his free hand

Flora, in her cornflower-blue dress, comes out from the interior

Flora Good-morning!

Das Miss Crewe! Here I am! A little late! Forgive me!

Flora I didn't realize — I've been writing a letter. Does this look all right?

Das (*nervously*) Very, very good.

Flora Now ... this will be nice, we'll both be working. Poet and painter. Work in progress.

Das unstraps his work-box and establishes himself on the verandah. Flora establishes herself at her work table. Pike is puzzling over a letter

Pike She says paint on paper.

Mrs Swan Yes.

Pike "... a smudge of paint on paper..." — "Perhaps my soul will stay behind as a smudge of paint on paper" ... She's referring to an actual painting, isn't she?

Mrs Swan I don't know.

Pike And "undressed". She says "undressed". Like a nude. On *paper*. That would be a watercolour, wouldn't it?

Mrs Swan What would? There isn't any "it".

Pike Well, if it doesn't mean a portrait of Flora undressed, what do you think it means?

Mrs Swan As much or as little as you like. Isn't that the point of being a poet?

Pike I don't know, I'm not a poet, but it reads quite specific, the deserted house ... where is the bit?

Mrs Swan Between your teeth, Eldon.

Pike Here. "In an empty house ..." — "Perhaps my soul will stay behind as a smudge of paint on paper, as if I'd always been here, like ... Radha?"

Mrs Swan Radha.

Pike "— the most beautiful of the herdswomen, undressed" ——

Mrs Swan (*interrupting, briskly*) Well, the portrait, as it happens, is on canvas and Flora is wearing her cornflower dress.

Pike Portrait?

Mrs Swan She mentions the portrait somewhere. It was rolled up in the suitcase.

Pike Eleanor ... do you mean there's a portrait of Flora?

Mrs Swan Would you like to see it?

Pike Oh my God.

Mrs Swan It's fairly ghastly, like an Indian cinema poster. I think I know where it is but I'll need you to get it down for me. Should we go in? We're about to lose the sun.

Pike Oh my God. But this is ... Oh my God. There's never been one, not a real portrait.

Mrs Swan That's true. Apart from the Paris portrait; but that was on canvas, too.

Pike The *Paris* portrait ... ?

Mrs Swan Yes, Flora's first time in Paris, she was driving an ambulance, officially, in the last year of the '14-'18 war ... so she was twenty-three, I suppose, when she met Modigliani.

Pike Modigliani?!

Mrs Swan Oh, Flora met everybody. Not that Modigliani was anybody at the time.

Pike A portrait by Modigliani?

Mrs Swan I was nine at the Armistice, so that was, my goodness, sixty-six years ago! I'm coming up to seventy-five, you know.

Pike Eleanor ... I can hardly believe my ears.

Mrs Swan I'm afraid so. I was born in 1909. But thank you, Eldon. Have another slice of cake.

Pike No — thank you — I — excuse me: a painting of Flora by Modigli ——

Mrs Swan Yes. A nude.

Pike (*reverently*) A nude!

Mrs Swan I never saw it myself. I was at school, of course, and then, it was too late.

Pike Too late?

Mrs Swan Yes, isn't that bad luck? The Technicolor Flora like a cork in a storm, washed up on top of a wardrobe in a bungalow in Shepperton, and the Modigliani, which would have paid for the bungalow several times over, burned to ashes in a bathtub in the Ritz.

By now she has assembled the tea-tray and she leaves with it

Pike Could you run that by me again?

Pike totters after her

Flora, in her blue dress, is at the table on the verandah, writing in her notebook with a fountain pen. She pauses, thinking, sitting quite still. Her feet are bare and her shoes are placed neatly to one side. Das is painting her portrait

Flora (*recorded*) "Yes I am in heat like a bride in a bath,
        without secrets, soaked in heated air
        that liquifies to the touch and floods,
        shortening the breath, yes
        I am discovered, heat has found me out,
        a stain that stops at nothing,
        not the squeezed gates or soft gutters,
        it slicks into the press
        that prints me to the sheet
        yes, think of a woman in a house of net
        that strains the oxygen out of the air
        thickening the night to Indian ink
        or think if you prefer — "

Flora has unconsciously crossed her legs, which brings Das's work to a halt. He waits, patiently. She notices that Das has stopped

  Oh ...
Das No, please be comfortable.
Flora I'm sorry! (*She puts her feet side-by-side*) There. Is that how I was?
Das You are patient with me. I think your nature is very kind.
Flora Do you think so, Mr Das?
Das I am sure of it. May I ask you a personal question?
Flora That is a personal question.
Das Oh my goodness, is it?
Flora I always think so. It always feels like one. Carte blanche is what you're asking, Mr Das. Am I to lay myself bare before you?
Das (*panicking slightly*) My question was only about your poem!
Flora At least you knew it was personal.
Das I will not ask it now, of course.
Flora On that understanding I will answer it. My poem is about heat.
Das Oh. Thank you.

Flora I resume my pose. Pen to paper. Legs uncrossed. You know, you are the first man to paint my toe-nails.

Das Actually, I am occupied in the folds of your skirt.

Flora Ah. In that you are not the first.

Das You have been painted before? — but of course you have! Many times, I expect!

Flora You know, Mr Das, your nature is much kinder than mine.

Flora resumes. Das resumes

Anish Das comes into the Shepperton garden. He has a soft briefcase; he sits in one of the garden chairs

Mr Das, I have been considering whether to ask you a delicate question, as between friends and artists.

Das Oh, Miss Crewe, I am transported beyond my most fantastical hopes of our fellowship! This is a red-letter day without dispute!

Flora If you are going to be so Indian I shan't ask it.

Das But I cannot be less Indian than I am.

Flora You could if you tried. I'm not sure I'm going to ask you now.

Das Then you need not, dear Miss Crewe! You considered. The unasked, the almost asked question, united us for a moment in its intimacy, we came together in your mind like a spark in a vacuum glass, and the redness of the day's letter will not be denied.

Flora You are still doing it, Mr Das.

Das You wish me to be less Indian?

Flora I did say that but I think what I meant was for you to be more Indian, or at any rate Indian, not Englished-up and all over me like a labrador and knocking things off tables with your tail — so waggish of you, Mr Das, to compare my mind to a vacuum. You only do it with us, I don't believe that left to yourself you can't have an ordinary conversation without jumping backwards through hoops of delight, with whoops of delight, I think I mean; actually, I do know what I mean, I want you to be with me as you would be if I were Indian.

Das An Indian Miss Crewe! Oh dear, that is a mental construction which has no counterpart in the material world.

Flora So is a unicorn, but you can imagine it.

Das You can imagine it but you cannot mount it.

Flora Imagining it was all I was asking in my case.

Das *(terribly discomfited)* Oh! Oh, my gracious! — I had no intention — I assure you ——

Flora *(amused)* No, no, you cannot unwag your very best wag. You cleared the table, the bric-à-brac is on the Wilton — the specimen vase, the snuff box, the souvenir of Broadstairs ——

But she has misjudged

Das (*anguished*) You are cruel to me, Miss Crewe!
Flora (*instantly repentant*) Oh! I'm so sorry. I didn't want to be. It's my
    nature. Please come out from behind your easel — look at me.
Das May we fall silent, please. I prefer to work in silence.
Flora I've spoiled everything. I'm very sorry.
Das The shadow has moved. I must correct it.
Flora Yes, it has moved. It cannot be corrected. We must wait for tomorrow.
    I'm so sorry.

*Das resumes working at the easel. Flora maintains her pose, but screws the
cap on to her fountain pen*

    *Mrs Swan comes from the bungalow with tea for two on a tray, and two
    kinds of cake*

Anish stands up at her approach

Anish Let me help you.
Mrs Swan I've forgotten your sugar.
Anish Actually, I don't take it.
Mrs Swan Oh. I thought you'd be more Indian.

They settle the tray and themselves at the garden table

Anish This is so kind of you.
Mrs Swan Oh no. Your letter was irresistible. Having an artist to tea was
    beyond my fondest hopes for my dotage. We'll let it sit a minute. Do you
    think you take after your father?
Anish I don't know. I would like to think so. But my father was a man who
    suffered for his beliefs and I have never had to do that, so perhaps I will
    never know.
Mrs Swan I really meant being a painter. You are a painter like your father.
Anish Oh ... yes. Yes, I am a painter like my father. Though not at all like
    my father, of course.
Mrs Swan Your father was an Indian painter, you mean?
Anish An Indian painter? Well, I'm as Indian as he was. But yes. I suppose
    I am not a particularly *Indian* painter ... not an Indian painter *particularly*,
    or rather ...
Mrs Swan Not particularly an Indian painter.
Anish Yes. But then, nor was he. Apart from being Indian.
Mrs Swan As you are.

Anish Yes.

Mrs Swan Though you are not at all like him.

Anish No. Yes. My father was a quite different kind of artist, a portrait painter, as you know ...

Mrs Swan I can't say I do, Mr Das. Until I received your letter your father was unknown to me. In fact, the attribution "Unknown Indian Artist" described the situation exactly ——

Anish He was not unknown in Jummapur!

Mrs Swan — if indeed it was your father who did the portrait of Flora.

Anish Oh, the portrait is certainly my father's work, Mrs Swan! You cannot imagine my feelings when I saw the book in the shop window — my excitement! You see, I carry my copy everywhere. (*He takes "The Collected Letters" from his briefcase. The dustjacket has the portrait of Flora by Nirad Das*)

Mrs Swan Well, I hope there'll be lots like you, Mr Das.

Anish There will be no-one like me, Mrs Swan! It was not the book, of course, but the painting on the jacket and reproduced inside. If only he could have known that one day his portrait of Flora Crewe ...

Mrs Swan He might have been more pleased to be in the window of an art gallery than a bookshop.

Anish Perhaps not. I'm sure my father never had a single one of his paintings reproduced, and that is an extraordinary pleasure for an artist. I know! The painting under one's hand is everything, of course ... unique. But replication! *That* is popularity! Put us on book jackets — calendars — biscuit tins! Oh, he would have been quite proud!

Mrs Swan By the way, what were your father's beliefs?

Anish (*surprised*) Why ... we are Hindu ...

Mrs Swan You said he had suffered for his beliefs.

Anish Oh. I meant his opinions.

Mrs Swan How did he suffer?

Anish He was put in prison.

Mrs Swan Really? By whom?

Anish Well, by you.

Mrs Swan By me? Oh ... by us. But how did we know what his opinions were?

Anish It seems he took part in some actions against the Raj during the Empire Day celebrations in Jummapur.

Mrs Swan Then he was put in prison for his actions, not his opinions, Mr Das, and obviously deserved what he got. Will you have a slice of cake?

Anish Thank you.

Mrs Swan Victoria sponge or Battenberg?

Anish Oh ...

Mrs Swan The sponge is my own, raspberry jam included.

Anish I would love some ... thank you.

Mrs Swan Tea? But all that must have been before you were born.

Anish Oh, yes, I was the child of my father's second marriage. I was born long after Independence, and my father went to prison in Jummapur in 1930.

Mrs Swan 1930! But that was when Flora was in Jummapur!

Anish Yes, I know. That is why I am here.

Mrs Swan administers tea

Flora takes the cap off her fountain pen

Flora Are we friends this morning?

Das I hope so! Why do you ask that? Has something happened?

Flora Oh. No.

She laughs. He frowns, painting

Well, I thought if we're friends I'll ask you to write something on the drawing you did of me. (*She produces the pencil sketch*)

Das Oh, but that was only a poor scribble! Not even a good likeness!

Flora Even so.

Das Oh. (*He is taken aback but then realizes he is being teased. He laughs*)

Flora Yes, you won't get anywhere with that.

Nazrul, the servant, brings a jug of fresh lemonade and two glasses, which he puts on the table

Namby pani time!

Nazrul Nimbupani!

Flora (*getting up*) Thank you, Nazrul ... Shukriya!

Nazrul responds and leaves

Das Actually, I have something for you, a little present.

Flora Have you? You mustn't keep giving me things, Mr Das!

Das Well, it is a kind of birthday present, you see.

Flora Especially not birthday presents when it isn't my birthday.

Das gives her an old but well-preserved book. It is green with a brown spine. In fact it is a copy of Up the Country *by Emily Eden [1866]*

Das I did not buy it, it is a book of my father's which I would like you to have. Letters by an English lady travelling in India a hundred years ago.

Flora (*truly pleased*) Oh, but this will be just my book! Thank you! *Up the Country* ... Emily Eden. Oh, it's a lovely present!

Das Well ... I will write, "To remind you of Jummapur and your friend and fellow artist Nirad Das". And I will draw myself listening to you.

Flora pours the nimbupani. Das writes on the pencil drawing with his own fountain pen, and settles down to draw her

Anish When my father met Flora Crewe he had been a widower for several years, although he was still quite a young man, younger than her, yes, the beginning of the Hot Weather in 1930 ... he had his 34th birthday on April 2nd, just after he met your sister. He had lost his wife to cholera and he was childless. I knew nothing of my father's life before me. In my earliest memory, my father was an old gentleman who spoke very little except when he sometimes read aloud to me. He liked to read in English. Robert Browning, Tennyson, Macaulay's *Lays of Ancient Rome*, and Dickens, of course ...

Mrs Swan How surprising.

Anish Oh yes — he went from a vernacular school to Elphinstone College in Bombay, and you only have to look at Elphinstone College to see that it was built to give us a proper English education.

Mrs Swan I meant, in view of his "opinions". But I spoke without thinking. Your father took part in actions against the British Raj and loved English literature, which was perfectly consistent of him.

Anish (*laughing*) Usually, the education succeeded admirably! In Jummapur we were "loyal" as you would say, we had been loyal to the British right through the first War of Independence.

Mrs Swan The ... ? What war was that?

Anish The Rising of 1857.

Mrs Swan Oh, you mean the Mutiny. What did you call it?

Anish Dear Mrs Swan, Imperial history is merely ... no, no — I promise you I didn't come to give you a history lesson.

Mrs Swan You seem ill-equipped to do so. We were your Romans, you know. We might have been your Normans.

Anish And did you expect us to be grateful?

Mrs Swan That's neither here nor there. I don't suppose I'd have been grateful if a lot of Romans turned up and started laying down the law and teaching Latin and so forth. "What a cheek," is probably what I would have thought. "Go away, and take your roads and your baths with you." It doesn't matter what I would have thought. It's what I think now that matters. You speak English better than most young people I meet. Did you go to school here?

Anish No, I went to a convent school in ... You are spreading a net for me, Mrs Swan!

Mrs Swan What net would that be? Have some more cake.

Anish Mrs Swan, you are a very wicked woman. You advance a preposterous argument and try to fill my mouth with cake so I cannot answer you. I will resist you and your cake. We were the Romans! We were up to date when you were a backward nation. The foreigners who invaded you found a third-world country! Even when you discovered India in the age of Shakespeare, we already had our Shakespeares. And our science — architecture — our literature and art, we had a culture older and more splendid, we were rich! After all, that's why you came.

But he has misjudged

Mrs Swan (*angrily*) We made you a proper country! And when we left you fell straight to pieces like Humpty Dumpty! Look at the map! You should feel nothing but shame!

Anish Oh, yes ... I am a guest here and I have been ...

Mrs Swan (*calming down*) No, only provocative. Will you be going home?

Anish (*bewildered*) I ... would you like me to go?

Mrs Swan (*equally bewildered*) No. What do you mean?

Anish (*understanding*) Oh — home! I didn't mean I was a guest in England. England is my home now. I have spent half my life here. I married here.

Mrs Swan An English girl?

Anish Yes. We met at art school.

Mrs Swan (*approvingly*) Artists together.

Anish Actually she was not a student, she was earning money as a model. Life class, you see.

Mrs Swan Of course. Is she still your model?

Anish No. My work is not figurative now.

Mrs Swan What is it now?

Anish Well, deconstructive.

Mrs Swan What a shame.

Anish I can still draw if I wish. May I draw you?

Mrs Swan Oh no, the last thing I need ——

Anish No, for myself.

Mrs Swan Oh. Why?

Anish Only a little sketch with a pencil. We must not resist when life strives to close one of its many circles!

Mrs Swan Is that Hinduism?

Anish Das Oh ... I don't know. Perhaps.

Mrs Swan Well, it sounds very east of Suez. All right then. You may draw me.

Anish It will make us friends.

Anish takes an artist's block from his briefcase and begins to draw her

Flora and Das sit at the table with lemonade

Flora While having tiffin on the verandah of my bungalow I spilled kedgeree on my dungarees and had to go to the gymkhana in my pyjamas looking like a coolie.

Das I was buying chutney in the bazaar when a thug escaped from the choky and killed a box-wallah for his loot, creating a hullabaloo and landing himself in the mulligatawny.

Flora I went doolally at the durbar and was sent back to Blighty in a dooley feeling rather dikki with a cup of char and a chit for a chotapeg.

Das Yes, and the burra sahib who looked so pukka in his topee sent a coolie to the memsahib ——

Flora No, no. You can't have memsahib and sahib that's cheating — and anyway I've already said coolie.

Das I concede, Miss Crewe. You are the Hobson-Jobson champion!

Flora You are chivalrous, Mr Das. So I'll confess I had help. I found a whole list of Anglo-Indian words in my bedside drawer, for the benefit of travellers.

Das But I know both languages, so you still win on handicap.

Flora Where did you learn everything, Mr Das?

Das From books. I like Dickens and Browning, and Shakespeare, of course — but my favourite is Agatha Christie! *The Mysterious Affair at Styles!* — oh, the woman is a genius! But I would like to write like Macaulay.

Flora Oh dear.

Das I have to thank Lord Macaulay for English, you know. It was his idea when he was in the government of India that English should be taught to us all. He wanted to supply the East India Company with clerks, but he was sowing dragon's teeth. Instead of babus he produced lawyers, journalists, civil servants, he produced Gandhi! We have so many, many languages, you know, that English is the only language the nationalists can communicate in! That is a very good joke on Macaulay, don't you think?

Flora Are you a nationalist, Mr Das?

Das *(lightly)* Ah, that is a very interesting question! But we shouldn't have stopped all this time. It's getting late for you, I must work more quickly tomorrow.

Flora It's only half-past ten.

Das No, it's already April, and that is becoming late.

Flora Yes, it seems hotter than ever. Would you like some more lemonade?

Das No, thank you, no lemonade. Miss Crewe, you haven't looked at my painting yet.

Flora No. Not yet. I never look. Do you mind?

Das No.

Flora You do really. But I once asked a painter "Can I look?" and he said, "Why? When I paint a table I don't have to show it to the table."

Das I said you had been painted before.

Flora Only once.

Das A portrait?

Flora Not in the way you mean. It was a nude.

Das Oh.

Flora Unusually. He painted his friends clothed. For nudes he used models. I believe I was his friend. But perhaps not. Perhaps a used model only. It hardly matters. He was dead so soon afterwards. (*Pause*) He was not so kind to me as you are.

Das Do you have the painting?

Flora No.

Das Where is it?

During the following we hear a horse. We do not see the horse

Flora Nowhere. A man I thought I might marry burned it. My goodness, what a red-letter day you are having. There's a man on a horse.

Durance (*off*) Good-morning! Miss Crewe, I think!

Flora (*standing up*) Yes — good-morning! (*To Das*) Do you know him?

Das He is the Assistant.

Durance (*off*) May I get down a moment?

Flora Of course. What a beautiful animal! (*To Das*) Assistant what?

Das (*to Flora*) Captain Durance!

Durance Thank you!

Flora Come on up, do join us.

Durance arrives on foot

Durance Oh — it's Mr Das, isn't it?

Das Good-morning, sir. But we have never met.

Durance Oh, but I know you. And Miss Crewe, your fame precedes you.

Flora Thank you ... and you ...

Durance I'm from the Residency. David Durance.

Flora (*shaking hands*) How do you do.

Durance Oh, but look here — I'm interrupting the artist.

Flora We had stopped.

Durance May one look? Oh, I say! Coming along jolly well! Don't you think so, Miss Crewe?

Das I must be going. I have overstayed my time today.

Flora But we'll continue tomorrow?

Das Yes. Perhaps a little earlier if it suits you. I can leave everything ... (*He prepares to remove the canvas from the easel*)

Flora Why don't you leave the canvas too? It will be quite safe.

Das (*hesitating*) Yes, all right ... I have a drape for it. Thank you. (*He drapes a cloth over the canvas on the easel*)

Flora Like shutting up the parrot for the night.

Das There we are. Thank you for the lemonade, Miss Crewe. An absolute treat. I promise you! Goodbye, sir — and — yes — and until tomorrow ...

Das goes down the verandah steps and wheels his bicycle away

Flora Yes ... goodbye! (*To Durance*) I'll put my shoes on. Sorry about my toes, but I like to wriggle them when I'm working.

Durance I'll only stay a moment. My chief asked me to look in. Just to make sure there's nothing we can do for you.

Flora Would you like some lemonade?

Durance No, nothing for me. Really. We might have found you more comfortable quarters, you know, not quite so in-the-town.

Flora How did you know I was here?

Durance Now, there's a point. Usually we know of arrivals because the first thing they do is drop in a card but in your case ... rumours in the bazaar, so to speak. Are you an old hand here, Miss Crewe?

Flora No, I've never been to India before. I came up from Bombay just a few days ago.

Durance But you have friends here, perhaps?

Flora No. I got on a ship and I came, knowing no-one. I have friends in England who have friends here. Actually, one friend.

Durance In Jummapur, this friend?

Flora No — the *friend* — my friend — is in London, of course; Mr Joshua Chamberlain. *His* friends are in different places in Rajputana, and I will also be going to Delhi and then up to the Punjab, I hope.

Durance Now I see. And your friend in London has friends in Jummapur.

Flora Yes.

Durance Like Mr Das?

Flora No. Are you a policeman of some kind. Mr Durance?

Durance Me? No. I'm sorry if I sound like one.

Flora Well, you do a bit. I'm travelling with letters of introduction to a number of social clubs and literary societies. I speak on the subject of "Literary Life in London", in return for board and lodging ... So you see I couldn't have taken advantage of your kindness without giving offence to my hosts.

Durance The game is different here. By putting up at the Residency you would have gained respect, not lost it.

Flora Thank you, but what about self-respect?

Durance Well ... as long as all is well. So you are following in Chamberlain's footsteps. All is explained.

Flora I don't think *I* explained it. But yes, I am. He spoke in Jummapur three years ago, on the subject of Empire.

Durance Yes. Is he a good friend?

Flora Well ...

Durance Did you know he was some sort of Communist?

Flora I thought he might be. He stood twice for Parliament as the Communist candidate.

Durance (*unoffended, pleasant as before*) I amuse you. That's all right, amusing our distinguished visitors is among my duties.

Flora Well, don't be so stuffy.

Durance How long will you be with us?

Flora I'm expected in Jaipur but they don't mind when I come.

Durance I'm sure you'll have a marvellous time. There are wonderful things to see. Meanwhile, please consider yourself an honorary member of the club — mention my name, but I'll put you in the book.

Flora Thank you.

Durance Well ...

He offer his hand and she shakes it

Flora Call again, if you like. I wish I had a lump of sugar for your horse. Next time.

Durance He's my main indulgence. I wish I'd been here when a good horse went with the job.

Flora Yes ... what is your job? You mentioned your chief.

Durance The Resident. He represents the government here.

Flora The British government?

Durance Delhi. The Viceroy, in fact. Jummapur is not British India ... you understand that?

Flora Yes ... but it's all the Empire, isn't it?

Durance Oh yes. Absolutely. But there's about five hundred Rajahs and Maharajahs and Nabobs and so on who run bits of it, well, nearly half of it, actually, by treaty. And we're here to make sure they don't get up to mischief.

Flora I knew you were a kind of policeman.

Durance laughs and goes down the steps of the verandah. He hesitates shyly

Durance Miss Crewe, would you have dinner with us while you are here?

Flora With you and your wife, do you mean?

Durance No ... at the club. Us. With me. I don't run to a wife, I'm afraid. But do come. We're a reasonably civilized lot, and there's usually dancing on Saturdays, only a gramophone but lots of fun.

Flora I'd love to. On Saturday, then.

Durance Oh ... splendid! I'll come by.

Flora I haven't got a horse, you know.

Durance We have a Daimler at the Residency. I'll see if I can wangle it. Pick you up about eight?

Flora Yes.

Durance We don't dress, normally, except on dress nights. (*He laughs at himself*) Obviously.

Flora I'll be ready.

Durance Jolly good.

He exits and mounts the horse which snorts

Flora Goodbye!

Durance (*off*) Goodbye!

Flora (*calling out*) Wangle the Daimler!

Flora waves and turns aside. She sits at her table and starts to write

During the following, Nazrul enters and removes the tray of glasses and jug of lemonade

Anish is drawing Mrs Swan

Mrs Swan But Jummapur was a Native State.

Anish Yes.

Mrs Swan So *we* didn't put your father in gaol.

Anish (*politely dissenting*) Ah well ...

Mrs Swan (*firmly*) Whatever your father may have done, the Resident would have had no authority to imprison an Indian. The Rajah of Jummapur had his own justice.

Anish Ah, but His Highness the Rajah ——

Mrs Swan Oh, I'm not saying we wouldn't have boxed his ears and sent him packing if he forgot which side his bread was buttered, but facts are facts. The Rajah put your father in the choky. How long for, by the way?

Anish Six months.

Mrs Swan There you are. In British India he would have got a year at least. After the War it may have been different. With Independence round the corner, people were queuing up to go to prison, it was their ticket to the top. They'd do their bit of civil disobedience and hop into the paddy-waggon

thoroughly pleased with themselves. Eric — that's my husband — would
let them off with a small fine if he thought they were Johnny-come-latelies
and they'd be furious. That was when Eric had his District. We were right
up near Nepal ...

Anish Yes, the tea-tray ...

Mrs Swan You spotted it. In India we had pictures of coaching inns and
foxhunting, and now I've landed up in Shepperton I've got elephants and
prayer wheels cluttering up the window ledges, and the tea-tray is Nepalese
brass. One could make a comment about human nature but have a slice of
Battenburg instead.

Anish Thank you.

Mrs Swan I got it specially, an artistic sort of cake, I always think. What kind
of paintings are they, these paintings that are not like your father's?
Describe your latest. Like the cake?

Anish (*eating*) Delicious. Thank you.

Mrs Swan No, are they like the cake?

Anish Oh. No. They are all ... like each other really. I can't describe them.

Mrs Swan Indescribable, then.

Anish completes the drawing, and passes it to her

Anish There.

Mrs Swan (*pleasantly surprised*) Ah. That's a proper drawing. You could
do portraits if you wanted.

She gives the drawing back to Anish

Anish Thank you.

Mrs Swan Now, what are we going to tell Eldon about your father?

Anish Eldon?

Mrs Swan E. Cooper Pike. He calls me Eleanor so I have to call him Eldon,
so as not to seem toffee-nosed. If he starts calling me Nell I suppose I'll
have to call him El. He's waiting for me to die so he can get on with Flora's
biography which he thinks I don't know he's writing.

Anish (*referring to his copy of the book*) Oh yes. "Edited by E. Cooper Pike."

Mrs Swan That means he does the footnotes.

Anish Oh yes, I see.

Mrs Swan Far too much of a good thing, in my opinion, the footnotes; to be
constantly interrupted by someone telling you things you already know or
don't need to know at that moment. There are pages where Flora can hardly
get a word in sideways. Mr Pike teaches Flora Crewe. It makes her sound
like a subject, doesn't it, like biology. Or in her case, botany. Flora is widely
taught in America. I have been written to, even visited, and on one occasion

telephoned, by young women doing Flora Crewe. Almost always young women. And from all over, lots from America. Flora has become quite a heroine. Which she always was to me. I was only three when Mother died, so it was Flora who ... Oh dear, I'm going to need a hanky.

Anish Oh — I say! I'm sorry ——

Mrs Swan Found it. (*She blows her nose*) It makes me so cross that she missed it all, the Collected Poems, and now the Letters, with her name all over the place and students and professors so interested and so sweet about her poetry. Nobody gave tuppence about her while she was alive except to get her knickers off. How is your tea?

Das arrives at the guesthouse and props his bicycle against the verandah

Flora, working, barely acknowledges him

Anish It's very nice. Mrs Swan ... it says, "The portrait of Flora Crewe is reproduced by permission of Mrs Eleanor Swan." Does that mean you have it?

Mrs Swan Yes.

Anish Here? In your house?

Mrs Swan Would you like to see it?

Anish Very much! I half expected to see it hanging the moment I arrived.

Mrs Swan That's because you're a painter. I'll bring it out. Yes, I can't get the tea here to taste as it should. I expect it's the water. A reservoir near Staines won't have the makings of a good cup of tea compared to the water we got in the Hills. It came straight off the Himalayas.

She leaves

Flora and Das are at work

Flora (*recorded*)
                    "... yes, think of a woman in a blue dress
                    sat on a straight-backed chair at a plain table
                    on the verandah of a guesthouse,
                    writing about the weather.
                    Or think, if you prefer, of bitches,
                    cats, goats, monkeys at it like" ——
Oh, fiddlesticks! May we stop for a moment. (*She gets up*) I'm sticking to myself.

Das Of course! Forgive me!

Flora You mustn't take responsibility for the climate too, Mr Das.

Das No, I ...

Flora No, I'm sorry. I'm bad tempered. Should we have some tea? I wouldn't mind something to eat too. (*Calling out*) Nazrul! (*To Das*) There's a jar of duck pâté in the refrigerator ...

Nazrul appears from round the corner of the verandah

Oh, Nazrul ... char and ...
Nazrul (*in Hindi*) Yes, madam, I will bring tea immediately ...
Flora ... bread ... and in the icebox, no, don't go, listen to me ——
Das Would you allow me, please?

Das and Nazrul speak in Hindi. Das orders bread and butter and the duck pâté from the fridge

Flora (*over the conversation*) A jar with a picture of a duck ...

But Nazrul has dramatic and tragic disclosures to make. Thieves have stolen the pâté. Das berates him. Nazrul leaves the way he came

What was all that?
Das He will bring tea, and bread and butter and cake. The pâté has been taken by robbers.
Flora What?!
Das (*gravely*) Just so, I'm afraid.
Flora But the refrigerator is padlocked — Mr Coomaraswami pointed it out to me particularly.
Das Where do you keep the key?
Flora Nazrul keeps it, of course.
Das Ah well ... the whole thing is a great mystery.

Flora splutters into laughter and Das joins in

Flora But surely, isn't it against his religion?
Das Oh, certainly. I should say so. Not that I'm saying Nazrul stole the pâté, but stealing would be against his religion, undoubtedly.
Flora I don't mean stealing, I mean the pork.
Das But I thought you said it was duck.
Flora One must read the small print, Mr Das. "Duck pâté" in large letters, "with pork" in small letters. It's normal commercial practice.
Das Yes, I see.
Flora We must hope he only got the duck part ——
Das That is your true nature speaking, Miss Crewe!
Flora — though of course, if they use one pig for every duck, he'll be lucky to have got any duck at all.

Das The truth will never be known, only to God who is merciful.

Flora Yes. Which God do you mean?

Das Yours if you wish, by all means.

Flora Now, Mr Das, there is such a thing as being too polite. Yours was here first.

Das Oh, but we Hindus can afford to be generous; we have gods to spare, one for every occasion. And Krishna said, "Whichever god a man worships, it is I who answers the prayer."

Flora I wasn't sure whether Krishna was a god or a person.

Das Oh, he was most certainly a god, one of the ten incarnations of Vishnu. He had a great love affair, you see, with a married lady, Radha.

Flora I think that's what confused me.

Das Radha was the most beautiful of the herdswomen. She fell passionately in love with Krishna. She would often escape from her husband to meet him in secret. It is a favourite subject of the old Rajasthani painters.

Flora Come and sit down, Mr Das.

Das I will ... but I will start on my tree while we wait.

Flora Put a monkey in it.

Das Yes. Like Hanuman, he is my favourite in the Ramayana. The monkey god.

Flora Mr Coomaraswami showed me the temples.

Das Did you find them interesting?

Flora I liked some of the sculptures, the way the women are often smiling to themselves. Yes, that was quite revealing, I thought.

Das About Indian women?

Flora No, about Indian sculptors. And breasts like melons, and baby-bearing hips. You must think me ill-favoured.

Das No. My wife was slightly built.

Flora Oh ...

Nazrul enters with the tea-tray

Thank you, Nazrul ... And two kinds of cake!

Nazrul replies smilingly and leaves

Das But your face today ... I think your work was troublesome.

Flora Yes.

Das Is it the rhyming that is difficult?

Flora No.

Das The metre?

Flora No. The ... emotion won't harmonize. I'm afraid I'm not much good at talking about it.

Das I'm sorry.

Flora That's why I don't keep nipping round to your side of the easel. If I don't look there's nothing to say. I think that that's better.

Das Yes. It is better to wait. My painting has no *rasa* today.

Flora What is *rasa*?

Das *Rasa* is juice. Its taste. Its essence. A painting must have its *rasa* ... which is not in the painting exactly. *Rasa* is what you must feel when you see a painting, or hear music; it is the emotion which the artist must arouse in you.

Flora And poetry? Does a poem have *rasa*?

Das Oh yes! Poetry is a sentence whose soul is *rasa*. That is a famous dictum of Vishvanata, a great teacher of poetry, six hundred years ago.

Flora *Rasa* ... yes. My poem has no *rasa*.

Das Or perhaps it has two *rasa* which are in conflict.

Flora Oh ...

Das There are nine *rasa*, each one a different colour. I should say mood. But each mood has its colour — white for laughter and fun, red for anger, pale yellow for tranquillity ——

Flora (*interrupting*) Oh ... is there one for grey?

Das Grey is for sorrow.

Flora Sorrow? I see.

Das Each one has its own name and its own god, too.

Flora And some don't get on, is that it?

Das Yes. That is it. Some do and some don't. If you arouse emotions which are in opposition to each other the *rasa* will not ... harmonize, you said.

Flora Yes.

Das Your poem is about heat.

Flora Yes.

Das But its *rasa* is perhaps ... anger?

Flora Sex.

Das (*unhesitatingly*) The *rasa* of erotic love is called Shringara. Its god is Vishnu, and its colour is *shyama*, which is blue-black. Vishvanata in his book on poetics tells us: Shringara requires, naturally, a lover and his loved one, who may be a courtesan if she is sincerely enamoured, and it is aroused by, for example, the moon, the scent of sandalwood, or being in an empty house. Shringara goes harmoniously with all other *rasa* and their complementary emotions, with the exception of fear, cruelty, disgust and sloth.

Flora I see. Thank you. Empty house is very good. Mr Das, you sounded just like somebody else. Yourself, I expect. I knew you could. The other one reminded me of Dr Aziz in Forster's novel. Have you read it? I kept wanting to kick him.

Das (*offended*) Oh ...

Flora For not knowing his worth.

Das Then perhaps you didn't finish it.
Flora Yes, perhaps. Does he improve?
Das He alters.
Flora What is your opinion of *A Passage To India*?
Das Was that the delicate question you considered to ask me?
Flora (*laughing happily*) Oh, Mr Das!

Pike enters, dressed for India. He is staying at the best hotel in Jummapur, and looks it. He carries a smart shoulder-bag. He stares around him in a vaguely disappointed way

Modern street sounds, including music from radios, etc., distinctly Indian, accompany Pike's entrance, then fade out

Flora is at her table, writing. Das is at the easel, painting

(*Writing*) "Jummapur, Saturday April 5th. Darling Nell. I'm having my portrait painted, I mean the painter is at it as I write, so if you see a picture of me in my cornflower dress you'll know I was writing *this* — some of the time anyway. He thinks I'm writing a poem. Posing as a poet, you see, just as the Enemy once said of me in his rotten rag."
Pike "The Enemy" was J. C. Squire (1884-1958), poet, critic, literary editor of the *New Statesman* and editor of the *London Mercury*. An anonymous editorial in the *London Mercury* (April 1920) complained about, "an outbreak of versifying flappers who should stop posing as poets and confine themselves to posing as railway stations". The magazine was sued by the poets Elizabeth Paddington (1901-1980) and Meredith Euston (1899-1929), both cases being settled out of court. FC poured a pint of beer over Squire's head in the Fitzroy Tavern in January 1921.

Dilip enters with a bottle of cola

Dilip Dr Pike ...
Pike Eldon, please.
Dilip ... will you have a cola, Eldon?
Pike Oh, thanks. What kind of ... (*His suspicion has been aroused*) *Thumbs Up* Cola? You know, I think maybe I won't.
Dilip (*misunderstanding*) I got two — really — I drank mine while I was talking to the shopkeeper. It is as I thought. The dak bungalow was exactly here, in the courtyard. Of course, the flats did not exist. I'm afraid nothing you can see goes back to before the war.
Pike No ... That's a shame.
Dilip Except the tree, perhaps.
Pike (*brightening*) Oh, yes. The tree. That's right. She mentions a tree.

Dilip The old man remembers the bungalow very well. It was destroyed. A casualty of Partition.

Pike Taken apart?

Dilip Burned, in the riots. There were many people killed here in '47.

Pike *Partition.* Oh, yes ... terrible ... Would this be the same tree?

Dilip Probably. It looks old.

Pike Would you take my picture?... on the spot.

Dilip Yes, certainly.

Pike This is so good of you, Dilip.

Dilip No, no, it is a red-letter day for the fellowship of teachers of English literature!

Pike takes a camera from his bag and gives it to Dilip

Pike It's self-focusing ... just press the ... (*He positions himself*) I could take out an ad ... in the newspaper. Someone may remember an artist ... Go back a bit ... show more of the ...

Dilip No, the 35 is fine. Do you mind if I take it off auto? ... stop it down for the background ... F8 ...

Pike Oh ... sure.

Dilip Yes, why not? — put an advert in the paper. Ready? (*He takes the photo*)

Pike Thank you. I'll take one of you.

Dilip All right. (*Adjusting the camera*) On 50. More of Dilip.

They change places, Pike taking the camera. Dilip has a bag from which he takes "The Collected Letters of Flora Crewe", to hold it for his photograph

After all ... fifty-six years ... he could be still alive ... he'd only have to be ...

Pike Ninety.

Dilip Yes, probably not. Is this all right?

Pike The other thing is ... What do I do?

Dilip Just point it.

Pike The other thing is, Dilip ... Here we go. (*He takes the picture*)

Dilip Thank you.

Pike The other thing is, there was the watercolour. A lost portrait, a nude. That's the way it reads to me. Don't you think so?

Dilip (*laughing*) Oh yes, I think that's the way it reads to you, Eldon, but she was a poet ... and you're a biographer! A lost portrait would be just the ticket.

Pike How about offering a reward?

Dilip A reward?

Pike For information leading to. If the local paper did a story about it ... I bet that would get results.

Dilip Undoubtedly. Your hotel will be stormed by a mob waving authentic watercolour portraits of English ladies in every stage of undress.

Pike I should get a shot from above, with the tree ... Could one get on the roof, do you think?

Dilip I'm sure. Let me go and see.

Dilip leaves

During the following, a couple of pi-dogs are heard yapping and barking

Flora "Darling, you musn't expect me to be Intelligence from Abroad. You obviously know much more about the Salt March than I do."

Pike Gandhi's "March to the Sea" to protest the Salt Tax began at Ahmedabad on March 12th. He reached the sea on the day this letter was written.

Flora "Nobody has mentioned it to me. If I remember I'll ask at the club tonight — I've had a visit from a clean young Englishman who asked me to dinner. It was a bit of an afterthought really. I think I made a gaffe by not announcing myself to the Resident, and the young man, he was on a horse, was sent to look me over. I think he ticked me off but he was so nice it was hard to tell. I've a feeling I'm going to have to stop in a minute. My artist is frowning at me and then at the canvas as if one of us is misbehaving. He is charming and eager and reminds me of Charlie Chaplin, not the idiotic one in the films, the real one who was at the Trees' lunch party."

Pike It was Sir Herbert Beerbohm Tree who, soon after the Crewe family arrived in London from Derbyshire, gave FC her first employment, fleetingly as a cockney bystander in the original production of *Pygmalion*, and, after objections from Mrs Patrick Campbell, more permanently "in the office". It was this connection which brought FC into the orbit of Tree's daughter Iris and her friend Nancy Cunard, and thence to the Sitwells, and arguably to the writing of poetry.

Flora "My poem, the one I'm not writing, is about sitting still and being hot. It got defeated by its subject matter, and I should be gone to the hills, I'm only waiting for my artist to finish. The Hot Weather, they tell me, is about to start, but I can't imagine anything hotter than this, and it will be followed by the Wet Season, though I already feel as though I'm sitting in a puddle. I don't think this is what Dr Guppy meant by a warm climate."

Pike Dr Alfred Guppy had been the Crewe family doctor since the move from Derbyshire to London in 1913. His notes on FC's illness, with reference to pulmonary congestion, are first dated 1926.

Flora Oh, shut up!

It is as though she has turned on Pike. Simultaneously, Das, losing his temper, is shouting in Hindi, "Get off! Get off!" But they are both shouting at the

unseen pi-dogs who are now fighting under the verandah. In the middle of
this, Dilip calls out for "Eldon!". The fuss resolves itself

   Pike follows Dilip off

The dogs go whining into oblivion

Das Oh — fiddlesticks!
Flora I'm sorry — is it my fault?
Das No — how can it be?
Flora Is that so silly?
Das No ... forgive me! Oh dear, Miss Crewe! Yesterday I felt ... a communion
   and today ——
Flora Oh! ... It is my fault! Yesterday I was writing a poem, and today I have
   been writing a letter to my sister. That's what it is.
Das A letter?
Flora I am not the same sitter. How thoughtless of me.
Das Yes. Yes.
Flora Are you angry ?
Das I don't know. Can we stop now? I would like a cigarette. Would you care
   for a cigarette? They are Gold Flake.
Flora No. But I'd like you to smoke.
Das Thank you. (*He lights a cigarette*) You were writing to your sister? She
   is in England, of course.
Flora Yes, in London. Her name is Eleanor. She is much younger than me.
Das And also beautiful like you?
Flora Routine gallantry is disappointing from you.
Das (*surprised*) Oh, it was not.
Flora Then, thank you.
Das Where does your sister live?
Flora That's almost the first thing you asked me. Would it mean anything
   to you?

Das is loosening up again, regaining his normal good nature

Das Oh, I have the whole of London spread out in my imagination. Challenge
   me, you will see!
Flora All right, she lives in Holborn.
Das (*after a pause*) Oh. Which part of London is that?
Flora Well, it's — oh dear — between the Gray's Inn Road and ——
Das Holl-born!
Flora Yes. Holborn.
Das But of course I know Holl-born! Charles Dickens lived in Doughty
   Street.

Flora Yes. Eleanor lives in Doughty Street.

Das But, Miss Crewe, Oliver Twist was written in that very street!

Flora Well, that's where Eleanor lives, over her work. She is the assistant to the editor of a weekly, *The Flag*.

Das *The Flag*?

Flora You surely have never read that too?

Das No, but I have met the editor of *The Flag* ——

Flora (*realizing*) Yes — of course you have! That is how I came to be here. Mr Chamberlain gave me letters of introduction.

Das His lecture in Jummapur caused the Theosophical Society to be suspended for one year.

Flora I'm sorry. But it's not for me to apologize for the Raj.

Das Oh, it was not the Raj but the Rajah! His Highness is not a socialist! Do you agree with Mr Chamberlain's theory of Empire? I was not persuaded. Of course I am not an economist.

Flora That has never deterred Mr Chamberlain.

Das It is not my opinion that England's imperial adventure is simply to buy time against revolution at home.

Flora Political opinions are often, and perhaps entirely, a function of temperament, Mr Das. Eleanor and Mr Chamberlain are well suited.

Das Your sister shares Mr Chamberlain's opinions?

Flora Naturally.

Das Being his assistant, you mean.

Flora His mistress.

Das Oh.

Flora You should have been a barrister, Mr Das.

Das I am justly rebuked!

Flora It was not a rebuke. An unintended slight, perhaps.

Das I am very sorry about your sister. It must be a great sadness for you.

Flora I am very happy for her.

Das But she will never be married now! Unless Mr Chamberlain marries her.

Flora He is already married, otherwise he might.

Das Oh my goodness. How different things are. Here, you see, your sister would have been cast out — for bringing shame on her father's house.

Flora snorts

Yes — perhaps we are not so enlightened as you.

Flora Yes, perhaps. Well, you have had your cigarette. Are we going to continue?

Das No, not today.

Flora I'll go back to my poem.

Das There is no need.

Flora Well, I'll copy out my poem for my sister. I do that for safe keeping, you see. I'm sending her the drawing you did of me at the lecture.

Das (*after a pause*) I have an appointment I had forgotten.

Flora Oh.

Das Actually you musn't feel obliged ... (*He begins gathering together his paraphernalia, apparently in a hurry now*)

Flora What have I done?

Das Done? What should you have done?

Flora Stop it. Please. Stop being Indian.

Das (*after a pause*) You have looked at the portrait, Miss Crewe?

Flora Oh, I see. Yes, yes ... I did look.

Das Yes.

Flora I had a peep. Why not? You wanted me to.

Das Yes, why not? You looked at the painting and you decided to spend the time writing letters. Why not?

Flora I'm sorry.

Das You still have said nothing about the painting.

Flora I know.

Das I cannot continue today.

Flora I understand. Will we try again tomorrow?

Das Tomorrow is Sunday.

Flora The next day.

Das Perhaps I cannot continue at all.

Flora Oh. And all because I said nothing. Are you at the mercy of every breeze that blows? Are you an artist at all?

Das Perhaps not! A mere sketcher — a hack painter who should be working in the bazaar!

He snatches up the "pencil sketch" from under Flora's hand

Flora (*realizing his intention*) Stop it!

Das tears the paper in half

Das Or in chalks on the ghat!

Flora Stop!

But Das tears the paper again, and again and again, until it is in small pieces

I'm ashamed of you!

Das Excuse me, please! I wish to leave. I will take the canvas ——

Flora You will not!

It becomes a physical tussle. A struggle. She begins to gasp

Das You need not see it again!
Flora You will not take anything! We will continue!
Das I do not want to continue, Miss Crewe. Please let go!
Flora I won't let you give up!
Das Let go, damn you, someone will see us!
Flora And stop crying! You're not a baby!
Das (*fighting her*) I will cry if I wish!
Flora Cry, then, but you will finish what you started! How else will you ever
  ... Oh!

And suddenly Flora is helpless, gasping for breath

Das Oh ... oh, Miss Crewe — oh my God — let me help you. I'm sorry.
  Please. Here, sit down ——

*She has had an attack of breathlessness. He helps her to a chair. Flora speaks
with difficulty*

Flora Really, I'm all right. (*Pause. She takes careful breaths*) There.
Das What happened?
Flora I'm not allowed to wrestle with people. It's a considerable nuisance.
  My lungs are bad, you see.
Das Let me move the cushion.
Flora It's all right. I'm back now. Panic over. I'm here for my health, you
  see. Well, not here ... I'll stay longer in the Hills.
Das Yes, that will be better. You must go high.
Flora Yes. In a day or two.
Das What is the matter with you?
Flora Oh, sloshing about inside. Can't breathe under water. I'm sorry if I
  frightened you.
Das You did frighten me.
Flora I'm soaking.
Das You must change your clothes.
Flora Yes. I'll go in now. I've got a shiver. Pull me up. Thank you. Ugh. I
  need to be rubbed down like a horse.
Das Perhaps some tea ... I'll go to the kitchen and tell ——
Flora Yes. Would you? I'll have a shower and get into my Wendy house.
Das Your ... ?
Flora My big towel is on the kitchen verandah — would you ask Nazrul to
  put it in the bedroom?

Das runs towards the kitchen verandah, shouting for Nazrul. Flora goes into the interior, into the bedroom, undressing as she goes, dropping the blue dress on the floor, and enters the bathroom in her underwear

Das returns, hurrying, with a white towel. He enters the interior cautiously, calling "Miss Crewe..." He enters the bedroom and finds it empty. From the bathroom there is the sound of the water pipes thumping, but no sound of water

Flora (*off*) Oh, damn, come on!
Das Miss Crewe ...

The thumping in the pipes continues

Das approaches the bathroom door

   (*Louder*) Miss Crewe! I'm sorry, there's no ——
Flora (*off, shouting*) There's no water!

The thumping noise continues

Das Miss Crewe! I'm sorry, the electricity ——

The thumping noise suddenly stops

   (*In mid-shout*) The electric pump ——

   Flora enters naked

Flora I have to lie down.
Das Oh! (*Thrusting the towel at her*) Oh, I'm so sorry!

Relieved of the towel, Das is frozen with horror

Flora I'm sorry, Mr Das, but really I feel too peculiar to mind at the moment.
Das (*turning to leave hurriedly*) Please forgive me!
Flora No, please, there's water in the jug on the wash-stand.

She stands shivering, hugging the towel

   Do be quick.
Das (*getting the water*) It's the electricity for the pump.
Flora Is there any water?

Das Yes, it's full ... Here ——

He gives her the jug, and turns away

Flora Thank you. No, you do it. Over my head, and my back, please.

Das pours the water over her, carefully

    Oh, heaven ... Oh, thank you ... I'm terribly sorry about this. Oh, that's good. Tip the last bit on the towel.
Das There ...

She wipes her face with the wet corner of the towel

Flora I feel as weak as a kitten.
Das I'm afraid that's all.
Flora Thank you. (*She wraps the towel around herself*) Could you do the net for me?

Das lifts one side of the mosquito net and Flora climbs on to the bed

    I'll be all right now.
Das (*misunderstanding; leaving*) Yes, of course.
Flora Mr Das, I think there's soda water in the refrigerator. Would you ...?
Das Oh yes. But is it locked? I cannot find Nazrul.
Flora Oh ... I'm already hot again. And no electricity for the fan. It's too late for modesty. (*She discards the towel and gets under the sheet*) Anyway, I'm your model.
Das I will fetch soda water from the shop.
Flora That was the thing I was going to ask you.
Das When?
Flora The delicate question ... whether you would prefer to paint me nude.
Das Oh.
Flora I preferred it. I had more what-do-you-call it.
Das *Rasa*.
Flora (*laughing quietly*) Yes, *rasa*.

Das leaves the bedroom and goes along the verandah towards the servants' quarters and disappears round the corner

Mrs Swan returns with Das's portrait of Flora. The canvas is inside a cardboard tube

Mrs Swan This is how it came back from the publishers. I tuck things away.
You hold her and I'll pull the tube.
Anish Thank you.
Mrs Swan Well, there she is.
Anish Oh ... !
Mrs Swan Yes, a bit much, isn't it?
Anish Oh ... it's so vibrant.
Mrs Swan Vibrant. Yes ... oh, you're not going to blub too, are you?
Anish (*weeping*) I'm sorry.
Mrs Swan Don't worry. Borrow my hanky ...

He takes her handkerchief

Anish Please excuse me ...
Mrs Swan It just goes to show, you need an eye. And your father, after all,
was, like you, an Indian painter.
Anish I'm sorry I ... you know.
Mrs Swan No, I should not have been disparaging. Let me see.

She takes the painting from Anish and looks at it

Yes, book jackets and biscuit tins are all very well, but obviously there's
something that stays behind in the painting after all.
Anish Yes. Even unfinished.
Mrs Swan Unfinished?
Anish It wasn't clear from the book, the way they cropped the painting. You
see where my father has only indicated the tree, and the monkey ... He
would have gone back to complete the background only when he consid-
ered the figure finished. Believe me. I wondered why he hadn't signed it.
Now I know. My father abandoned this portrait.
Mrs Swan Why?
Anish He began another one.
Mrs Swan How do you know, Mr Das?
Anish Because I have it.

*He opens his briefcase and withdraws the watercolour which is hardly larger
than the page of a book, protected by stiff boards. He shows her the painting
which is described in the text*

Mrs Swan Oh heavens! Oh ... yes ... *of course.* How like Flora.
Anish More than a good likeness, Mrs Swan.
Mrs Swan No ... I mean, *how like Flora!*

She continues to look at the painting

Nazrul returns to the dak bungalow, with shopping, the worse for wear, disappearing towards the kitchen area

Das starts shouting at him and Nazrul is heard protesting

Das returns to view with a bottle of soda water. He speaks first from outside the bedroom

Das Nazrul has returned, most fortunately. I was able to unlock the refrigerator. I have soda water.
Flora Thank you, Mr Das!

Das enters the bedroom

Das (*approaching the bed*) Should I pour the water for you?

On the little table by the bed, outside the mosquito net, there is a glass with a beaded lace cover. Das pours the water

Nazrul was delayed at the shops by a riot, he says. The police charged the mob with lathis, he could have easily been killed, but by heroism and inspired by his loyalty to the memsahib he managed to return only an hour late with all the food you gave him money for except two chickens which were torn from his grasp.
Flora Oh dear ... you thanked him, I hope.
Das I struck him, of course. You should fine him for the chickens.

Flora lifts the net sufficiently to take the glass from Das, who then steps back rather further than necessary

Flora (*drinking*) Oh, that's nice. It's still cold. Perhaps there really was a riot.
Das Oh yes. Very probably. I have sent Nazrul to fetch the dhobi — you must have fresh linen for the bed. Nazrul will bring water but you must not drink it.
Flora Thank you.

The punkah begins to flap quite slowly, a regular beat

Das I'm sure the electricity will return soon and the fan will be working.
Flora What's that? Oh, the punkah!
Das I have found a boy to be punkah-wallah.
Flora Yes, it makes a draught. Thank you. A little boy?
Das Don't worry about him. I've told him the memsahib is sick.

Flora The memsahib. Oh dear.

Das Yes, you are memsahib. Are you all right now, Miss Crewe?

Flora Oh yes. I'm only shamming now.

Das May I return later to make certain?

Flora Are you leaving now? Yes, I've made you late.

Das No, not at all. There is no-one waiting for me. But the servant will return and ... we Indians are frightful gossips, you see.

Flora Oh.

Das It is for yourself, not me.

Flora I don't believe you, Mr Das, not entirely.

Das To tell you the truth, this is the first time I have been alone in a room with an Englishwoman.

Flora Oh. Well, you certainly started at the deep end.

Das We need not refer to it again. It was a calamity.

Flora (*amused*) A calamity! That's not spoken like an artist.

Das Then perhaps I am not an artist, as you said.

Flora I did not. All I did was hold my tongue and you had a tantrum. What would you have done in the rough and tumble of literary life in London? I expect you would have hanged yourself by now. When *Nymph in Her Orisons* came out one of the reviewers called it *Nymph In Her Mania*, as if my poems which I had found so hard to write were a kind of dalliance, no more than that. I met my critic somewhere a few months later and poured his drink over his head and went home and wrote a poem. So that was all right. But he'd taken weeks away from me and I mind that now.

Das Oh! — you're not dying are you?!

Flora I expect so, but I intend to take years and years about it. You'll be dead too, one day, so let me be a lesson to you. Learn to take no notice. I said nothing about your painting, if you want to know, because I thought you'd be an Indian artist.

Das An Indian artist?

Flora Yes. You *are* an Indian artist, aren't you? Stick up for yourself. Why do you like everything English?

Das I do not like everything English.

Flora Yes, you do. You're enthralled. Chelsea, Bloomsbury, Oliver Twist, Gold Flake cigarettes, Winsor and Newton ... even painting in oils, that's not Indian. You're trying to paint me from my point of view instead of yours — what you *think* is my point of view. You *deserve* the bloody Empire!

Das (*sharply*) May I sit down please?

Flora Yes, do. Flora is herself again.

Das I will move the chair near the door.

Flora You can move the chair on to the verandah if you like, so the servants won't ——

Das I would like to smoke, that is what I meant.

Flora Oh. I'm sorry. Thank you. In that case, can you see me through the net from over there?

Das Barely.

Flora Is that no or yes? (*She raises the sheet off her body and flaps it like a sail and lets it settle again*) Oof! — that's better! That's what I love about my little house — you can see out better than you can see in.

Das (*passionately*) But you are looking at such a house! The bloody Empire finished off Indian painting!

Pause

Excuse me.

Flora No, that's better.

Das Perhaps your sister is right. And Mr Chamberlain. Perhaps we have been robbed. Yes; when the books are balanced. The women here wear saris made in Lancashire. The cotton is Indian but we cannot compete in the weaving. Mr Chamberlain explained it all to us in simple Marxist language. Actually, he caused some offence. He didn't realize we had Marxists of our own, many of them in the Jummapur Theosophical Society.

Flora Mr Coomaraswami ... ?

Das No, not Mr Coomaraswami. *His* criticism is that you haven't exploited India *enough*. "Where are the cotton mills? The steel mills? No investment, no planning. The Empire has failed us!" That is Mr Coomaraswami. Well, the Empire will one day be gone like the Mughal Empire before it, and only their monuments remain — the visions of Shah Jahan! — of Sir Edwin Lutyens!

Flora "Look on my works, ye mighty, and despair!"

Das (*delighted*) Oh yes! Finally like the empire of Ozymandias! Entirely forgotten except in a poem by an English poet. You see how privileged we are, Miss Crewe. Only in art can empires cheat oblivion, because only the artist can say, "Look on my works, ye mighty, and despair!"

Flora I just didn't like you thinking English was better because it was English. Can't you paint me without thinking of Rossetti or Millais? Especially without thinking of Holman Hunt. Did you consider my question?

Das When you stood ... with the pitcher of water, you were an Alma-Tadema.

Flora Well, I don't want to be painted like that either.

Das I don't understand why you are angry with me.

Flora You were painting me as a gift, to please me.

Das Yes. Yes, it was a gift for you.

Flora If you don't start learning to *take* you'll never be shot of us. *Who whom.* Nothing else counts. Mr Chamberlain is bosh. Mr Coomaraswami is bosh.

It's your country, and we've got it. Everything else is bosh. When I was
Modi's model I might as well have *been* a table. When he was done, he got
rid of me. There was no question who whom. You'd never change his
colour on a map. But please light your Gold Flake.

Pause. Das lights his cigarette with a match

Das I like the Pre-Raphaelites because they tell stories. That is my tradition,
too. I am Rajasthani. Our art is narrative art, stories from the legends and
romances. The English painters had the Bible and Shakespeare, King
Arthur ... We had the Bhagavata Purana, and the Rasikpriya which was
written exactly when Shakespeare had his first play. And long before
Chaucer we had the Chaurapanchasika, from Kashmir, which is poems of
love written by the poet of the court on his way to his execution for falling
in love with the king's daughter, and the king liked the poems so very much
he pardoned the poet and allowed the lovers to marry.
Flora Oh ...
Das But the favourite book of the Rajput painters was the Gita Govinda
which tells the story of Krishna and Radha the most beautiful of the
herdswomen.

The ceiling fan starts working

Flora The electricity is on.
Das You will be a little cooler now.
Flora Yes. I might have a sleep.
Das That would be good.
Flora Mr Durance has invited me to dinner at the club.
Das Will you be well enough?
Flora I am well now.
Das That is good. Goodbye, then.
Flora Were Krishna and Radha punished in the story?
Das What for?
Flora I should have come here years ago. The punkah boy can stop now. Will
you give him a rupee? I'll return it tomorrow.
Das I will give him an anna. A rupee would upset the market.

Das leaves

Flora remains in the bed

CURTAIN

ACT II

The Jummapur Club after sundown

Gramophone music. Three couples are dancing: Flora and Durance, the Resident and the Englishwoman, and a third couple, an Englishman and English Lady

Somewhat removed from the dance floor is a verandah, which is spacious enough not only for the necessary furniture but also for two gymnasium horses, fitted out with stirrups and reins. These "horses" are used for practising polo swings and there are indeed a couple of polo sticks, a couple of topees and odd bits of gear lying in the corner

Pike is sitting alone on the verandah. He is tieless, wearing a Lacoste-type short-sleeved sports shirt

Englishwoman Are you writing a poem about India, Flora?

Flora Trying to!

Englishman Kipling — there's a poet! "Though I've belted you and flayed you, by the living Gawd that made you, you're a better man than I am Gunga Din!"

Englishwoman Gerald. You're showing us up. Flora writes *modern* poetry, don't you, dear, not the sort people can *remember*.

Flora Oh, but I like all kinds.

Resident The only poet I *know* is Alfred Housman. I expect you've come across him.

Flora (*pleased*) Oh yes, indeed I have!

Resident A dry old stick, isn't he?

Flora Oh — come *across him* ——

Resident He hauled me though "Ars Amatoria" when I was up at Trinity.

Flora (*pleased*) Oh, yes — the Art of Love!

Resident When it comes to love, Housman said, you're either an Ovid man or a Virgil man — *omnia vincit amor et nos cedamus amori* — you can't win against love; we give in to it. That's Virgil. Housman was an Ovid man — *et mihi cedet amor* — "Love won't win against me!"

Flora I'm a Virgil man.

Resident Are you? Well, you make friends more quickly that way.

Englishwoman Will you be here for the Queen's Ball, Flora?

Flora The ... ?

Englishwoman It comes off next month, Queen Victoria's birthday, and there's the gymkhana!

Flora Oh ... I can't, I'm afraid. I'll be going up the country soon; is that the expression?

Resident Of course, you're here on doctor's orders, I believe.

Flora Why ... yes ...

Resident If there's anything you need or want you tell David—right, David?

Durance Yes, sir.

Flora Thank you. He's already promised me a go in the Daimler.

Durance (*embarrassed*) Oh ... Flora's keen on autos.

Englishwoman If you like cars, His Highness has got about eighty-six of them. Collects them like stamps.

Flora His Highness?

Englishman The Rajah of Jummapur. The collectingness is terrific.

Another record begins to play

Resident Well, don't let us stop you enjoying yourselves.

Durance Would you like to dance, Flora?

Flora I'm out of puff. Do you think there might be more air outside?

Durance On the verandah? Any air that's going. Should we take a peg with us?

The Kipling fan, unseen, is singing "On the Road to Mandalay"

The dancers disperse. Durance and Flora go

Dilip, now smartly dressed in a jacket and tie, enters the verandah from within, in something of a hurry, carrying a jacket and a tie. The jacket is a faded beige gabardine with metal buttons, the skimpy jacket of a servant. On the breast, however, not instantly apparent, is a short strip of grimy campaign ribbons

Dilip Here I am at last! — I am so sorry, my fault entirely for not thinking to mention—but, look—all will be well in a jiffy!—and I have terrifically good news.

Pike (*getting up*) Thank you, Dilip — what ...?

Dilip (*helping him on with the jacket, which is too small for Pike*) Put it on and I will tell you. The jacket is a miserable garment, and our benefactor, I'm afraid, isn't quite your size.

Pike (*implausibly*) This is fine.

Dilip The tie, on the other hand, is tip-top, Jummapur Cricket Club. My friend Mr Balvinder Lal keeps a small stock on the premises. I spared you the blazer.

Pike obligingly starts putting on the striped tie

Pike Do you mean you can't come in here without a jacket and tie, not ever?

Dilip Not in the dining-room after sunset. Oh these rules are absurd! But — Eldon — something wonderful has come of it. I have discovered the name of your painter!

Pike You *have*?

Dilip I have! His name was Nirad Das. Now we can *research*!

Pike But Dilip — but that's ... how did you ... ?

Dilip It was God. If you had been wearing a jacket we would still be in the dark. But in borrowing the jacket, you see — oh, don't think that I discuss your affairs — it only seemed, shall I say, tactical to point out your distinction ——

Pike Dilip, never mind about that ——

Dilip Nor, for that matter, was the owner of the jacket indulging in impertinent curiosity about your private business, I assure you — actually, I know him well, he is an Old Soldier, formerly in the 6th Rajputana Rifles ——

Pike Dilip — *please*!

Dilip He remembers the English lady who stayed in the dak house.

Pike Who remembers?

Dilip The owner of this jacket.

Pike He ... he *remembers* ... ? But are you sure it was the same — ?

Dilip Oh yes — he saw Miss Crewe having her portrait painted.

Pike (*when he recovers*) I have to talk to him.

Dilip Of course. After dinner we will ——

Pike *After dinner*? He could *die* while I'm eating! Where is he? Ask him to have dinner with us.

Dilip Oh, that is not possible, you see.

Pike Why not?

Dilip He would not like that. Anyway, he does not have a jacket.

Pike We're getting off the point there ——

Dilip Also, he is working now.

Pike What, he works here?

Dilip Exactly. He works here. He is in charge of supervising the cloakroom.

Pike Well, that's wonderful. Show me the way.

Dilip Eldon, please be guided by me. We will not rush at the fences in the lavatory. (*He points at the ribbons on Pike's breast*) One of these is the ribbon for '39 to '45. This one, I think, is the Burma Star. He is without one leg. He has no sons. He has three daughters, two of them unmarried and to marry the third he sold his army pension and secured for himself a job which is cleaning toilets. Tomorrow there is time, there is reflection, there is ... esteem ... We can take a cup of tea together on the *maidan* and talk of old times. Believe me.

Pike Esteem. If he dies I'll kill you.

Dilip (*laughing*) He will not die. Let me go and see if our table's ready. Oh, how terrible — ! With all this excitement I have not offered you an aperitif.

Pike What's his name, Dilip?

Dilip Mr Ram Sunil Singh, formerly Subadar, B Company, 6th Rajputana Rifles.

Pike He must be pretty ancient.

The gramophone music creeps back in

Flora, alone, comes out on to the verandah

Dilip No, not at all. He was only a small boy, you see. One day the memsahib was sick and Ram Sunil Singh worked the punkah to cool the air. Mr Nirad Das gave him two annas. One does not forget such things. (*Leaving now*) I won't be a jiff. I must say, I could eat a horse!

Dilip leaves

Flora "My suitor — I suppose I must call him that, though I swear I've done nothing to encourage him — came to fetch me in an open Daimler which drew such a crowd, and off we went with people practically falling off the mud-guards, rather like leaving Bow Street — my God, how strange, that was ten years ago almost to the day."

Pike In fact, nine. See "The Woman Who Wrote What She Knew", E. C. Pike, *Modern Language Review*, Spring 1979.

Flora "And everyone at the club was very friendly, going out of their way to explain that although they didn't go in much for poetry, they had nothing against it, so that was all right, and dinner was soup, boiled fish, lamb cutlets, sherry trifle and sardines on toast, and it beats me how we're getting away with it, darling, I wouldn't trust some of them to run the *Hackney* Empire. Well, it's all going to end. That's official. I heard it from the horse's mouth ——"

The Resident and the Englishwoman dance into view, in a cheerful mood

Resident (*dancing*) (a) It is our moral duty to remain and (b) we will shirk it.

The Resident and the Englishwoman, dancing, spin out of view

Durance appears now, followed by a Servant with two tumblers of whisky and a soda syphon on a salver

Durance Here we are. Two burra-pegs.
Flora Lots of soda with mine, please.
Durance I'll do it.

The Servant bows and leaves

Dilip reappears

Dilip Eldon! We can eat! I hope you will like my club. The Jummapur Palace is a beautiful hotel, naturally, but *this* was the place in the old days when the palace was still the private residence of the Rajah.
Pike (*following him out*) Where does he live now?
Dilip (*leaving*) In the penthouse! The fish curry is usually good, and on no account miss the bread-and-butter pudding!

Dilip and Pike go

Durance Say when. (*He deals with the drinks*)
Flora When ... Cheers.
Durance Cheers.
Flora I'm sorry I packed up on you.
Durance This is nicer. So you've come to India for your health ...
Flora Is that amusing?
Durance Well, it is rather. Have you seen the English cemetery?
Flora No.
Durance I must take you there.
Flora Oh.
Durance People here drop like flies — cholera, typhoid, malaria — men, women and children, here one day, gone the next. Are you sure the doctor said India?
Flora He didn't say India. He said a sea voyage and somewhere warm. I wanted to come to India.
Durance Good for you. Live dangerously. In a month, you can't imagine it, the heat. But you'll be gone to the hills, so you'll be all right. (*Referring to the chair*) There we are. Long-sleever. Good for putting the feet up.
Flora Yes — long-sleever. Thank you. It's a nice club.
Durance Yes, it's decent enough. There are not so many British here so we tend to mix more.
Flora With the Indians?
Durance No. In India proper, I mean our India, there'd be two or three clubs.

The box-wallahs would have their own and the government people would stick together, you know how it is — and the Army ...

Flora Mr Das called you Captain.

Durance Yes, I'm Army. Seconded, of course. There are two of us juniors — political agents we call ourselves when we're on tour round the States. Jummapur is not one of your twenty-one-gun salute states, you see — my chief is in charge of half a dozen native states.

Flora In charge?

Durance Oh yes.

Flora Is he Army? No — how silly ——

Durance He's Indian Civil Service. The heaven-born. A Brahmin.

Flora Not seriously?

Durance Yes, seriously. Oh no, not a Brahmin seriously. But it might come to that with I-zation.

Flora ... ?

Durance Indianization. It's all over, you know. We have Indian officers in the Regiment now. My fellow Junior here is Indian, too, terribly nice chap — he's ICS, passed the exam, did his year at Cambridge, learned polo and knives-and-forks, and here he is, a pukkah sahib in the Indian Civil Service.

Flora Is he here?

Durance At the Club? No, he can't come into the club.

Flora Oh.

Durance Cheers. Your health, Flora. I drink to your health, for which you came. I wish you were staying longer. I mean, only for my sake, Flora.

Flora Yes, but I'm not. So that's that. Don't look hangdog. You might like me less and less as you got to know me.

Durance Will you come riding in the morning?

Flora Seriously.

Durance Yes, seriously. Will you?

Flora In the Daimler?

Durance No. Say you will. We'll have to go inside in a minute if no-one comes out.

Flora Why?

Durance There's nothing to do here except gossip, you see. They're all agog about you. One of the wives claims ... Were you in the papers at home? Some scandal about one of your books, something like that?

Flora I can see why you're nervous, being trapped out here with me — let's go in ——

Durance No — I'm sorry. Flora ... ? Pax? Please.

Flora All right, Pax.

He kisses her, uninvited, tentatively

Durance Sealed with a kiss.

Flora No more. I mean it, David. Think of your career.

Durance Are you really a scandalous woman?

Flora I was for a while. I was up in court, you know. Bow Street.

Durance (*alarmed*) Oh, not really?

Flora Almost really. I was a witness. The publisher was in the dock, but it was my poems — my first book.

Durance Oh, I say.

Flora The case was dismissed on a technicality, and the policemen were awfully sweet, they got me away through the crowd in a van. My sister was asked to leave school. But that was mostly my own fault — the magistrate asked me why all the poems seemed to be about sex, and I said, "Write what you know" — just showing off. I was practically a virgin, but it got me so thoroughly into the newspapers my name rings a bell even with the wife of a bloody jute planter or something in the middle of Rajputana, damn, damn, damn, no, let's go inside.

Durance Sit down, that's an order.

Durance, who has been standing, swings himself aboard one of the gymnasium horses

Flora Oh dear, you're not going to be masterful, are you?

Durance (*laughing*) Do you like polo?

Flora Well, I don't play a lot.

Durance Measure your swing, you see ... (*He swings the polo mallet*) How's your whisky?

Flora Excellent. All the better for being forbidden. My God, where did that moon come from?

Durance Better. I love this country, don't you?

Flora What's going to happen to it? The riot in town this morning ... does that happen often?

Durance Not here, no. The jails are filling up in British India.

Flora Well, then.

Durance It wasn't against us, it was Hindu and Moslem. Gandhi's Salt March reached the sea today, did you hear?

Flora No. I want to know.

Durance Our Congress Hindus closed their shops in sympathy, and the Moslems wouldn't join in, that's all it was about.

Flora My cook came home minus two chickens.

Durance The Indian National Congress is all very well, but to the Moslems, Congress means Gandhi ... a Hindu party in all but name.

Flora Will Gandhi be arrested?

Durance No, no. The Salt Tax is a lot of nonsense actually. It works out at about four annas a year. Most Indians didn't even know there was a Salt Tax.

Flora Well, they do now.
Durance Yes. They do now.
Flora Let me have a go.

There is a solar topee on the second horse. She puts the topee on her head, and puts her foot in the stirrup. Durance, laughing, helps Flora to heave herself on board the second horse

Oh yes, nothing to it. Yes, I can see the point of this, what fun, polo and knives-and-forks. Is that all you need to govern India?
Durance (*laughing*) Oh yes. There's about four of our chaps for every million Indians.
Flora Why do the Indians let us?
Durance Why not? We're better at it.
Flora Are we?
Durance Ask them.
Flora Who?
Durance The natives. Ask them. We've pulled this country together. It's taken a couple of hundred years with a hiccup or two but the place now works.
Flora That's what you love, then? What you created?
Durance Oh no — it's India I love. I'll show you.

The horses whinny. Flora's horse lurches just enough to almost throw her. She squeals, quite happily

The scene becomes exterior. The actors remain astride the gym horses

Ground mist

The horses whinny, the riders shift and rebalance themselves, Flora whooping with alarm, and birds are crying out, distancing rapidly

Sand grouse! Are you all right?
Flora They startled me.
Durance Time to trot.
Flora Oops — David — I'll have to tell you — stop! It's my first time on a horse, you see.
Durance Yes, I could tell.
Flora (*miffed*) Could you? Even walking? I felt so proud when we were walking.
Durance No, no good, I'm afraid.
Flora Oh, damn you. I'm going to get off.

Durance No, no, just sit. He's a chair. Breathe in. India smells wonderful,
doesn't it?

Flora Out here it does.

Durance You should smell chapattis cooking on a camel-dung fire out in the
Thar Desert. Perfume!

Flora What were you doing out there?

Durance Cooking chapattis on a camel-dung fire. (*He laughs*) I'll tell you
where it all went wrong with us and India. It was the Suez Canal. It let the
women in.

Flora Oh!

Durance Absolutely. When you had to sail round the Cape this was a man's
country and we mucked in with the natives. The memsahibs put a stop to
that. The memsahib won't muck in, won't even be alone in a room with an
Indian.

Flora Oh ...

Durance Don't point your toes out. May I ask you a personal question?

Flora No.

Durance All right.

Flora I wanted to ask *you* something. How did the Resident know I came to
India for my health?

Durance It's his business to know. Shoulders back. Reins too slack.

Flora But I didn't tell anybody.

Durance Obviously you did.

Flora Only Mr Das.

Durance Oh well, there you are. Jolly friendly of you, of course, sharing a
confidence, lemonade, all that, but they can't help themselves bragging
about it.

Flora (*furious*) Rubbish!

Durance Well ... I stand corrected.

Flora I'm sorry. I don't believe you, though.

Durance Righto.

Flora I'm sorry. Pax.

Durance Flora.

Flora No.

Durance Would you marry me?

Flora No.

Durance Would you think about it?

Flora No. Thank you.

Durance Love at first sight, you see. Forgive me.

Flora Oh, David.

Durance Knees together.

Flora 'Fraid so.

She laughs without malice but unrestrainedly. The horses trot

Dilip and Pike are in the garden/courtyard of the Jummapur Palace Hotel, which was formerly the Palace of the Rajah of Jummapur. They are brought drinks — reassuringly American cola — served by a Waiter decked out in the authentic livery of the old regime

Thus, the Servants operate freely between the two periods

Flora and Durance have gone

Dilip Poor Mr Nirad Das! Six months in the choky for throwing a mango!

Pike It's wonderful, Dilip. Subadar Ram Sunil Singh the toilet cleaner is a goldmine!

Dilip And he thinks you are one! How satisfactory.

Pike Did I give him too much? The poverty here is so ... Like the beggars at the traffic lights ... I started off shoving rupees, you know, through the window ... But it gets impossible. You can't ... there's more of them than you can ever ... I mean there's nothing to be in between, you have to be St Francis or some rich bastard who ignores them, there's nothing between that can touch it, the problem. Not St Francis, I didn't mean any disrespect, they're not *birds* — but Mother Teresa, some kind of saint. I lock the doors now. That's the truth. First thing I do now when the taxi hits a red light, I check the doors, wind up the window. But this one, she had this baby at the breast, I mean she looked *sixty*, and — well, this is the thing, she had a stump, you see, she had no hand, just this stump, up against the glass, and it was raw so when the light changed, the stump left this smear ...

Dilip You have to understand that begging is a profession. Like dentistry. Like shining shoes. It's a service. Every so often, you need to get a tooth filled, or your shoes shined, or to give alms. So when a beggar presents himself to you, you have to ask yourself — do I need a beggar today? If you do, give him alms. If you don't, don't. You have beggars in America.

Pike We have bums, winos, people down on their luck ... it's not a *service*, for God's sake.

Dilip Ah well, we are in a higher stage of development.

Pike Is that Hinduism, Dilip?

Dilip (*kindly*) It was a witticism, Eldon.

Pike Oh ... right.

Dilip One can see why the Theosophical Society transplanted itself from America. (*With his drink*) Let's drink to Madame Blavatsky.

Pike Who's she?

Dilip What? Don't you know "Bagpipe Music"?

Pike Oh ... (yeah).

Dilip "It's no go the yogi man, it's no go Blavatsky" ...

Pike MacNeice, right.

Dilip Madame Blavatsky was a famous name in India, she *was* the Theosophical Society. Of course, she was long dead by 1930, and now long forgotten, except in my favourite poem in the Oxford Book of English Verse.

Pike Why are you so crazy about English, Dilip?

Dilip I'm not!

Pike You love it!

Dilip Yes, I do. I love it.

Pike Yes. You do.

Dilip (*cheerfully*) Yes, it's a disaster for us! Fifty years of Independence and we are still hypnotized! Jackets and ties must be worn! English-model public schools for the children of the élite, and the voice of Bush House is heard in the land. Gandhi would fast again, I think. Only, this time he'd die. It was not for this India, I think, that your Nirad Das and his friends held up their home-made banner at the Empire Day gymkhana. It was not for this that he threw his mango at the Resident's car. What a pity, though, that all his revolutionary spirit went into his life and none into his art.

Pike Do you think he had a relationship with Flora Crewe?

Dilip But of course — a portrait is a relationship.

Pike No, a *relationship*.

Dilip I don't understand you.

Pike He painted her nude.

Dilip I don't think so.

Pike Somebody did.

Dilip In 1930, an Englishwoman, an Indian painter ... it is out of the question.

Pike Not if they had a relationship.

Dilip Oh ... a *relationship*? Is that what you say? (*Amused*) A relationship!

Pike This is serious.

Dilip (*laughing*) Oh, it's very serious. What do you say for — well, for "relationship"?

Pike Buddies.

Dilip almost falls off his chair with merriment

Please. Dilip ...

Dilip (*recovering*) Well, we will never know. You are constructing an edifice of speculation on a smudge of paint on paper, which no longer exists.

Pike It must exist — look how far I've come to find it.

Dilip Oh, very Indian! Well, if so, there are two ways to proceed. First, you can go around Jummapur looking at every piece of paper you come to. Second, you can stand in one place and look at every piece of paper that comes to you.

A Waiter brings a note to Pike, and leaves

Pike (*reading the note*) He's coming down. I thought maybe he'd ask us up to the penthouse.
Dilip Don't be offended.
Pike I'm not offended.
Dilip He is not the Rajah now, he is an ordinary politician. He has your letter. I hope he can help you. In any case, it is better if I leave you so he does not need to wear two hats.
Pike What do I call him?
Dilip Your Highness. He will correct you.

Dilip leaves

Flora enters, dressed for tiffin with his Highness the Rajah of Jummapur

Flora "I was let off church parade, being a suspected Bolshie, and I was writing on my verandah after my early-morning ride when what should turn up but a Rolls Royce circa 1912 but brand new, as it were, with a note from his Highness the Rajah of Jummapur going on about my spiritual beauty and inviting me to tiffin."

The Rajah enters

Rajah The spiritual beauty of Jummapur has been increased a thousandfold by your presence, Miss Crewe!
Flora "Well, what is a poor girl to do? Hop into the back of the Rolls, that's what."

The Rajah shakes hands with Flora who has stood up

Rajah How delightful that you were able to come! I understand you are a connoisseur of the automobile.
Flora Oh, how sweet of you to ask me ... Your Highness.
Rajah Unfortunately I cannot show them all at once because I have many more motor cars than mechanics, of course. But we can sit and chat between the scenes.
Flora I would be happy to walk around them, Your Highness.
Rajah Oh, but that would deny them their spiritual essence. They would not be automobiles if we did the moving and they did the sitting.

A stately concours d'élégance of motor cars, as distinguished as they are invisible, begins to pass in front of them

Flora Oh — ! What a beauty! A Duesenberg! And what's that? — Oh, my goodness, it's a Type 41 Bugatti! I've never seen one! And a ... is it an Isotta-Fraschini?

Rajah Possibly. I acquired it by way of settlement of a gambling debt at Bendor Westminster's. Do you know him?
Flora I don't know any dukes.
Rajah He's my neighbour in the South of France. I go to the South of France every year, you see, for my health. (*He laughs*) But *you* have come to India for your health!
Flora (*not pleased*) Well ... yes, Your Highness. Everybody seems to know everything about me.
Rajah Mr Churchill was in Bendor's house party. He paints. Like your friend Mr Das. Do you know Mr Churchill?
Flora Not very well.
Rajah I was at school with him, apparently. I can't remember him at all. But I read Mr Churchill's speeches with great interest, and ... oh — look at that one! I couldn't resist the headlamps. So enormous, like the eggs of a chromium bird.
Flora Yes — a Brancusi!
Rajah You know them all, Miss Crewe! ... Yes, Mr Churchill is perfectly right, don't you agree, Miss Crewe?
Flora About what exactly, Your Highness?
Rajah In his own words, the loss of India would reduce Britain to a minor power.
Flora That may be, but one must consider India's interests, too.
Rajah I must consider Jummapur's interests.
Flora Yes, of course, but aren't they the same thing?
Rajah No, no. Independence would be the beginning of the end for the Princely States. Though in a sense you are right, too — Independence will be the end of the unity of the Subcontinent. Look at the hullabaloo in the town yesterday. You tell Mr Churchill from me, Miss Crewe. My grandfather stood firm with the British during the First Uprising.
Flora The ... ?
Rajah In 1857 the danger was from fundamentalists ——
Flora The Mutiny ...
Rajah — today it is the progressives. No offence, Miss Crewe!
Flora I take it as a compliment.
Rajah Marxism. Civil disobedience. But I told the Viceroy, you have to fight them the same way, you won't win by playing cricket.

There is a pause in the cavalcade of motor cars

A Servant appears with a tray of drinks, fruit, a cigarette box, finger bowls and napkins

Ah, the first interval. Do you smoke? No? I enjoy a cigarette. You must tell me when you have had enough of automobiles. There are one or two things in my apartments which have drawn favourable comment from historians of Indian art, even exclamations of delight if I may be honest with you. Do you enjoy art, Miss Crewe?

Flora Frequently.

Rajah But of course you do, you are a poet. I would be happy to show you.

Flora I would like that very much.

Rajah You would really? Yes, I can see you are a true seeker. My ancestors' atelier produced some work which in my opinion compares with the best workshops of Rajasthan.

Flora I would like to see everything!

Rajah So you shall. Well, not quite everything, perhaps. Some of the most exquisite work, alas, is considered indelicate.

Flora Considered by whom? By you?

Rajah Oh no. In my culture, you see, erotic art has a long history and a most serious purpose.

Flora (*unangrily*) But only for men, Your Highness?

Rajah I have made you angry. I am terribly sorry. I should not have mentioned it.

Flora I'm very glad you did. Otherwise I should not have seen it.

Rajah (*comfortably*) Oh, my dear Miss Crewe, you are making me uncomfortable! What can I say?

Flora What do you usually say, Your Highness? Well ... here are some more cars ... I'm going to leave it to you.

Another car purrs by in front of them

(*Pleased*) Oh — a Silver Ghost. Goodness, that's beautiful.

Rajah Will you not have some fruit, Miss Crewe?

Flora Yes, I think I might. Thank you.

From the tray, which is piled up with tangerines, bananas, lychees, etc., she takes an apricot. She bites into it

Apricot is my favourite word.

Rajah Miss Crewe, you shall see all the paintings you wish to see; on the condition that you allow me to choose one to present to you.

Flora Oh ... thank you, Your Highness, but if there are going to be conditions, I'm not sure I want to see any.

Rajah The English ladies came, Mrs Tuke, Mrs Stokely-Smith, Mrs Blane ... a dozen of them, to see the lily pools, the flower garden ... They drank tea with me and I offered them fruit, but they would only eat the fruit which had a skin they could remove, you see.

Flora Yes, I see. Then I accept.

The next car has a distinct musical horn, which makes Flora gasp and almost jump out of her chair

Oh! — I know that one!
Rajah Of course you do, Miss Crewel
Flora No, I really know it. Where did you get it?
Rajah Well ... from a car shop.
Flora Could you make him stop a moment.

Flora stands up. The Rajah signals for the car to stop and it does so, idling. Flora takes a step or two towards the unseen car

Flora "And oh my darling, it was Gus's Bentley! I mean it was absolutely the one I broke my engagement in when I took Gus to the French paintings at Heal's — it still had the A B number-plate!"
Rajah It has memories for you, Miss Crewe?
Flora Yes, it does. Can I go and sit in it?
Rajah Romantic memories?
Flora The Tottenham Court Road, ten years ago. I hit a man with my shoe in that car.

Flora, going to the car, leaves the stage

Pike Augustus de Boucheron enjoyed brief celebrity as a millionaire philanthropist and patron of the arts. FC met him — and received his proposal of marriage — on December 3rd 1917. The occasion was Modigliani's first show, in Paris. FC sat for the artist soon afterwards. At the exhibition of Modern French Art at Heal and Sons in the Tottenham Court Road, London, in August 1919, Modigliani was one of several newer artists shown with the better known Matisse, Picasso and Derain. FC arrived at Heal's with de Boucheron, expecting to see her portrait, but before they got out of the Bentley she discovered that her fiancé had bought the painting from the artist and, as he triumphantly confessed, taken it back to the Ritz Hotel and burned it in a bathtub. In the ensuing row, FC returned de Boucheron's engagement ring, and made plans to sit for Modigliani again in the autumn of that year. But she delayed, arriving in Paris only on the morning of January 23rd, unaware that Modigliani had been taken to hospital. He died on the following evening, without regaining consciousness, of tuberculosis, aged thirty-five. De Boucheron, under his real name Perkins Butcher, went to prison in 1925 for issuing a false prospectus. His end is unknown.

The Rajah looks around the courtyard seeking someone ... and spots Pike. Pike has not noticed him. The Rajah, soi disant, approaches Pike

Rajah Professor Pike ... ?
Pike (*jumping up*) Oh! — indeed, yes — thank you.
Rajah (*shaking hands*) How do you do.
Pike An honour, sir.
Rajah (*waving Pike back into his chair*) Please ... I'm so sorry to have kept you waiting. But what I say is, a punctual politician is a politician who does not have enough to do. In other words, an impossibility.
Pike I'm so grateful to you for this.
Rajah No, no — delighted. I hope you find the hotel comfortable? We are not one of the international chains, you know. You mustn't be deluded on that point, no matter how much we exert ourselves to delude you.
Pike The hotel is excellent, Your Highness.
Rajah Actually, I am not "Your Highness", I am, in fact, just one of 542 members of the Lok Sabha, the House of the People, popularly elected, I am happy to say, by this District. Thank you so much for your book. I have already read the Indian letters. Perhaps you are wondering what happened to my grandfather's motor cars.
Pike No, I hadn't really ... What did happen to them?
Rajah My father presented them to the war effort. I can't think what he had in mind. Despatches carried by Rolls Royce, Staff Officers reporting for duty in snazzy Italian racing models ... But by that time the collection had suffered the attrition of my grandfather's generosity. He gave several away, sometimes as farewell presents to his lady friends. Which brings me to your letter. To begin with, there was a disappointment. There is no Flora Crewe in the visitors book in April 1930. However, my archivist has excelled himself. (*He takes a letter from his pocket*) The *Collected Letters* are not complete!
Pike A letter from Flora?
Rajah A thank-you note.
Pike May I?

The Rajah gives him the letter and waits while Pike reads it

He gave her a painting.
Rajah I believe we have identified it. Or rather, the volume from which it came. A miniature. From our Gita Govinda of about 1790, artist unknown. The series is by no means complete, but even so, I wish my grandfather had given her a motor car.
Pike Thank you. Yes, indeed.

He gives the letter back

Rajah I had a copy made for you.

The Rajah gives Pike the copy of the letter

Pike Thank you. That was thoughtful of you. The Gita Govinda ... would that be anything to do with a herdswoman, Radha?
Rajah But absolutely. It is the story of Radha and Krishna.
Pike Yes. And ... erotic? She could have been nude?
Rajah Well, let us say, knowing His Highness, the painting would have been appropriate to the occasion.
Pike A watercolour, of course. On paper.
Rajah Are you not feeling well, Professor Pike?
Pike No, I'm fine. Thank you. Actually, I'm not "Professor", I'm just one of the English Faculty ... Please call me Eldon.
Rajah (*getting up*) Well, Eldon ... I hope I have been of some service to your biography of Miss Crewe.
Pike Yes. You could say that. But thanks anyway. (*Correcting*) A lot. Thanks a lot. (*Remembering himself*) Thank you, Your Highness. (*Correcting*) Sir.

They shake hands

Rajah (*in Hindi*) Namaste!
Pike Is that your Christian name?
Rajah Actually, I am not Christian. No, I was saying goodbye. (*In Hindi*) Namaste!

The Rajah goes

Pike (*alone; rebuking himself under his breath*) Oh, great.

Pike goes

Mrs Swan and Anish are sitting in the garden with gin-and-tonic. Mrs Swan is looking at the watercolour. Anish is looking at the Rajah's gift to Flora

Mrs Swan I was a shandy drinker until I went out. G-and-T takes me right back to Rawalpindi. The bottles used to say *Indian* tonic water. I was quite surprised to discover when Eric got home leave that it was Indian everywhere, and always had been. Quinine, you see. Very good for staving off malaria, though interestingly quite useless, it seemed, without the gin. Eric swore by it, the gin part, he pointed out how it got dozens of our friends through malaria until their livers gave out. Then he had a stroke on the cricket field, silly goose, umpiring without a hat.

*Anish and Mrs Swan exchange watercolours, each one being returned to its
owner*

Anish From the Gita Govinda. Late eighteenth century, I think.

Mrs Swan It was in her suitcase.

Anish Mine was in my father's trunk.

Mrs Swan I didn't tell Eldon. He's not family.

Anish Thank you. I was in England when my father died. It was Christmas
Day. My first Christmas in London, in a house of student bedsits in
Ladbroke Grove. An unhappy day. All the other students had gone home
to their families, naturally. I was the only one left. No-one had invited me.

Mrs Swan Well, having a Hindu for Christmas can be tricky. Eric would
invite his Assistant for Christmas Day lunch. It quite spoiled the business
of the paper hats. There's nothing like wearing a paper hat with an Indian
at table for making one feel like a complete ass.

Anish The telephone rang all day.

Mrs Swan The mistletoe was another problem.

Anish It would stop and then start again. I ignored it. The phone was never
for me. But finally I went up and answered it, and it was my uncle calling
from Jummapur to say my father was dead.

Mrs Swan Oh, and at Christmas!

Anish I went home. It was still "home". I learned that my father had left me
his tin trunk which had always stood at the foot of his bed. There was
nothing of value in the trunk that I could see. It was full of paper, letters,
certificates, school report cards... (*He takes a newspaper clipping from his
wallet and gives it to Mrs Swan*) There was a newspaper cutting, however
— a report of a trial of three men accused of conspiring to cause a
disturbance at the Empire Day celebrations in Jummapur in 1930. My
father's name was there.

Mrs Swan (*reading*) "Nirad Das, aged 34."

Anish That is how I know the year. His birthday was in April and Empire
Day was in May.

Mrs Swan May the 24th, Queen Victoria's birthday.

Anish This is how I found out. My father never told me.

Mrs Swan And this painting?

Anish Yes. Underneath everything was this painting. A portrait of a woman,
nude, but in a composition in the old Rajasthani style. Even more amazing,
a European woman. I couldn't imagine who she was or what it meant. I kept
it, of course, all these years. Then, a week ago, in the shop window ... It was
like seeing a ghost. Not her ghost; his. It was my father's hand, his work,
I had grown up watching him work. I had seen a hundred original Nirad
Dases, and here was his work, not once but repeated twenty times over, a
special display. *The Collected Letters of Flora Crewe*, and I saw that it was
the same woman.

Mrs Swan Yes. Oh yes, it's Flora. It's as particular as an English miniature. A watercolour, isn't it?

Anish Watercolour and gouache.

Mrs Swan He hasn't made *her* Indian.

Anish Well, she was *not* Indian.

Mrs Swan Yes, I know, I'm not gaga, I'm only old. I mean he hasn't painted her flat. Everything else looks Indian, like enamel ... the moon and stars done with a pastry cutter. The birds singing in the border ... and the tree in bloom, so bright. Is it day or night? And everything on different scales. You can't tell if the painter is in the house or outside looking in.

Anish She is in a house within a house. The Mughals brought miniature painting from Persia, but Muslim and Hindu art are different. The Muslim artists were realists. But to us Hindus, everything is to be interpreted in the language of symbols.

Mrs Swan And a book on the pillow, that's Flora.

Anish Yes. That is her. Also the flowering vine ... look where it sheds its leaves and petals, they are falling to the ground. I think my father knew your sister was dying.

Mrs Swan Oh ...

Anish She is not posing, you see, but resting.

Mrs Swan Resting?

Anish This was painted with love. The vine embraces the dark trunk of the tree.

Mrs Swan Now really, Mr Das, sometimes a vine is only a vine. Whether she posed for him or whether it's a work of the imagination ...

Anish Oh, but the symbolism ——

Mrs Swan Codswallop! Your "house within a house", as anyone can see, is a mosquito net. And the book is Emily Eden, it was in her suitcase. Green with a brown spine. You should read the footnotes!

Mrs Swan and Anish leave as Pike enters

Pike The book was *Up the Country* (1866). Miss Eden was accompanying her brother, the Governor-General Lord Auckland, on an official progress up country. The tour, supported by a caravan of ten thousand people, including Auckland's French chef, lasted thirty months, and Emily wrote hundreds of letters home, happily unaware that the expedition was to set the stage for the greatest military disaster ever to befall the British under arms, the destruction of the army in Afghanistan.

Nirad Das and Coomaraswami are sitting on Flora's verandah. It is evening, nearly dark. They have not lit the lamp. A car is heard delivering Flora back to the guesthouse. Possibly the sweep of the headlights shows Das and Coomaraswami rising to greet Flora

She approaches the verandah, dark again, not seeing them and is startled

Flora Oh, Mr Das!
Das Good-evening, Miss Crewe! I'm sorry if we frightened you.
Flora And Mr Coomaraswami!
Coomaraswami Yes, it is me, Miss Crewe.
Flora Good-evening. What a surprise.
Coomaraswami I assure you — I beg you — we have not come to presume
  on your hospitality ——
Flora I wish I had some whisky to offer you, but will you come inside.
Coomaraswami It will be cooler for you to remain on the verandah.
Flora Let me find Nazrul.
Coomaraswami He is not here, evidently. But perhaps now that the mistress
  has returned it is permitted to light the lamp?
Flora Yes, of course.
Coomaraswami So much more pleasant than sitting in the electric light.

Coomaraswami lights the oil lamp

There we are. And the moon will clear the house-tops in a few minutes ...
Flora Please sit down.
Coomaraswami May I take this chair?
Flora No, that's Mr Das's chair. And this is mine. So that leaves you with
  the sofa.
Coomaraswami (*sitting down*) Oh yes, very comfortable. Thank you, Miss
  Crewe. Mr Das told me that I was exceeding our rights of acquaintance
  with you in coming to see you without proper arrangement, and even more
  so to lie in wait for you like *mulaquatis*. If it is so, he is blameless. Please
  direct your displeasure to me.
Das Miss Crewe does not understand *mulaquatis*.
Coomaraswami Petitioners!
Flora In this house you are always friends.
Coomaraswami Mr Das, what did I tell you!
Flora But what can I do for you?
Das Nothing at all! We require nothing!
Flora Oh ...
Coomaraswami Have you had a pleasant day, Miss Crewe?
Flora Extremely interesting. I have been visiting His Highness the Rajah.
Coomaraswami My goodness!
Flora I believe you knew that, Mr Coomaraswami.
Coomaraswami Oh, you have found me out!
Flora He showed me his cars ... and we had an interesting conversation,
  about art ...
Coomaraswami And poetry, of course.

Flora And politics.

Coomaraswami Politics, yes. I hope, we both hope — that your association with, that our association with, in fact — if you thought for a moment that I personally would have knowingly brought upon you, compromised you, by association with ——

Flora Stop, stop. Mr Das, I am going to ask *you*. What is the matter?

Das The matter?

Flora I shall be absolutely furious in a moment.

Das Yes, yes, quite so. My friend Coomaraswami, speaking as President of the Theosophical Society, wishes to say that if His Highness reproached you or engaged you in any unwelcome conversation regarding your connection with the Society, he feels responsible, and yet at the same time wishes you to know that ——

Flora His Highness never mentioned the Theosophical Society.

Das Ah.

Coomaraswami Not at all, Miss Crewe?

Flora Not at all.

Coomaraswami Oh ... well, jolly good!

Flora What has happened?

Coomaraswami Ah well, it is really of no interest. I am very sorry to have mentioned it. And we must leave you, it was not right to trouble you after all. Will you come, Mr Das?

Flora I hope it is nothing to do with my lecture?

Coomaraswami (*getting up*) Oh no! Certainly not!

Das Nothing!

Coomaraswami Mr Das said we should not mention the thing, and how truly he spoke. I am sorry. Good-night, Miss Crewe ——

Coomaraswami shouts towards somebody distant, in Hindi, and the explanation is an approaching jingle of harness, horse and buggy

Coomaraswami goes off to meet it

Das I am coming, Mr Coomaraswami. Please wait for me a moment.

Flora If you expect to be my friends, you must behave like friends and not like whatever-you-called-it. Tell me what has happened.

Coomaraswami (*off*) Mr Das!

Das (*shouting*) Please wait!

Flora Well?

Das The Theosophical Society has been suspended, you see. The order came to Mr Coomaraswami's house last night.

Flora But why?

Das Because of the disturbances in the town.

Flora The riot?

Das Yes, the riot.

Flora I know about it. The Hindus wanted the Moslems to close their shops. What has that to do with the Theosophical Society?

Coomaraswami (*off*) I am going, Mr Das!

Das (*shouting*) I come now! (*To Flora*) It is all bosh! The Theosophical Society is bosh! His Highness the Rajah is bosh! I must leave you, Miss Crewe. (*He hesitates*) I think I will not be coming tomorrow. Do you mind if I fetch my painting away now?

Flora I think that's up to you, Mr Das. I put everything inside.

Das asks permission to put on the electric light

Das May I?

He starts gathering his possessions. Flora turns down the oil lamp

Flora I think I should leave tomorrow.

Das Tomorrow?

Flora I think I must. Every day seems hotter than the day before.

Das Yes, you are right of course.

Flora Mr Das, did you tell people I was ill?

Das What do you mean?

Flora That I came to India for my health?

Coomaraswami (*more distant*) I cannot wait, Mr Das!

Das (*shouting*) A moment! (*To Flora*) Why do you ask me that?

Flora He is leaving you behind.

The horse and buggy are heard departing

Das I will walk, then.

Flora It seems that everyone from the Rajah to the Resident knows all about me. I told no-one except you. If I want people to know things, I tell them myself, you see. I'm sorry to mention it but if there's something wrong between two friends I always think it is better to say what it is.

Das Oh ... my dear Miss Crewe ... it was known to all long before you arrived in Jummapur. Mr Chamberlain's letter said exactly why you were coming. This is how it is with us, I'm afraid. The information was not considered to be private, only something to be treated with tact.

Flora Oh ...

Das As for the Rajah and the Resident, I am sure they knew before anybody. A letter from England to Mr Coomaraswami would certainly be opened.

Flora Oh ...

Das is embarrassed by her tears

Das You must not blame yourself. Please.
Flora Oh, Mr Das ... I'm so glad ... and so sorry. How idiotic I am. Have you got a hanky?
Das Yes ... certainly ...
Flora Thank you. And now I have made you walk. Leave everything here.
Das It is not far and the moon is rising, I can manage everything without difficulty.

He brings the easel and his box on to the verandah and returns for the canvas

Flora Mr Das. Don't take it. (*Pause*) If it is still a gift, I would like to keep it, just as it is.
Das Unfinished?
Flora Yes. To remind me of my friend and fellow artist Nirad Das. Your handkerchief smells faintly of... something nice.
Das The portrait is yours, if you would like it, of course. I must take it off the stretcher for you, or it will not travel easily in your luggage. Perhaps I can find a knife in the kitchen, to take out the little nails.
Flora There are scissors on the table.
Das Ah, yes. Thank you. No — I think I would damage them. May I call Nazrul?
Flora I thought ——
Das Yes — Mr Coomaraswami sent him away. He is suspicious of everyone. I'm sorry.
Flora It doesn't matter.

A power cut. All the lights go out. The scene continues in moonlight

Oh! The electricity again!
Das Yes. It is Jummapur, I'm afraid.
Flora Never mind.
Das Will we meet again?
Flora Perhaps, if I come back this way. I must be in Bombay by July the 10th at the latest. My ship sails on the 11th.
Das You may take a later ship.
Flora No, I cannot. My sister ... oh, you'll be horrified, but never mind — my sister is having a baby in October.
Das That is joyful news.
Flora Oh good.
Das Miss Crewe ... actually, I have brought something to show you which

I have made ... If we are friends again ... I would like you to see it.
Flora Then I would like to see it.

Das takes a small watercolour out of his pocket

Das I can light the lamp.
Flora There is enough light. Mr Coomaraswami was quite right about the
moon. (*She unwraps the paper*) It's going to be a drawing, isn't it? ... Oh!
Das (*nervous, bright*) Yes! A good joke, is it not? A Rajput miniature, by
Nirad Das!
Flora (*not heeding him*) Oh ... it's the most beautiful thing ...
Das (*brightly*) I'm so pleased you like it! A quite witty pastiche ——
Flora (*heeding him now*) Are you going to be Indian? Please don't.
Das (*heeding her*) I ... I am Indian.
Flora An Indian artist.
Das Yes.
Flora Yes. This one is for yourself.
Das Yes. You are not offended?
Flora No, I'm pleased. It has *rasa*.
Das I think so. Yes. I hope so.
Flora I forget its name.
Das (*after a pause*) Shringara.
Flora Yes. Shringara. The *rasa* of erotic love. Whose god is Vishnu.
Das Yes.
Flora Whose colour is blue-black.
Das Shyama. Yes.
Flora It seemed a strange colour for love.
Das Krishna was often painted shyama.
Flora Yes. I can see that now. It's the colour he looked in the moonlight.

They stand still, and in the moment the moonlight clouds to darkness

  Das exits

Flora undresses and lies inside the mosquito net

Flora (*recorded*)
             "Heat collects and holds as a pearl at my throat,
             lets go and slides like a tongue-tip down a Modigliani,
             spills into the delta, now in the salt-lick,
             lost in the mangroves and the airless moisture,
             a seed-pearl returning to the oyster —
             et nos cedamus amori ..."

Dawn

Approaching unseen, Pike and Dilip enter chanting

Pike
Dilip } *(together)* "It's no go the merrygoround, it's no go the rickshaw,
All we want is a limousine and a ticket for the peepshow.
Their knickers are made of crêpe de Chine, their shoes are made of python,
Their halls are lined with tiger rugs, and their walls with heads of bison."

It is dawn for them, too. They have been up all night. They each have a bottle of beer. They are happy, not drunk

Pike
Dilip } *(together)* "It's no go the yogi-man, it's no go Blavatsky,
All we want is a bank balance and a bit of skirt in a taxi!"

Pike *(toasting)* Madame Blavatsky and Louis MacNeice!

Dilip *(toasting)* Madame Blavatsky and the Theosophical Society, coupled with Indian nationalism!

Pike Really?

Dilip Oh yes. That's why the Jummapur branch was suppressed. The study of Indian religions is a very fine thing, no doubt, but politics is always the baby in the bathwater. Excuse me, I'll have a little rest.

Dilip lies on the ground on his back

Pike It's no go the records of the Theosophical Society, it's no go the newspaper files partitioned to ashes ... All we want is the facts and to tell the truth in our fashion ... Her knickers were made of crêpe de Chine, her poems were up in Bow Street, her list of friends laid end to end ... weren't in it for the poetry. But it's no go the watercolour, it's no go the Modigliani ... The glass is falling hour-by-hour, and we're back in the mulligatawny ... But we will leave no Das unturned. He had a son. God, this country is so *big*! — Dilip ...?

Dilip is asleep. Pike shakes him

Dilip! It's morning!

Dilip wakes refreshed

Dilip Ah yes. Would you like to come home for breakfast?

Pike Oh ... Thanks!

Dilip It's going to be hot today.

Pike It's hot every day.
Dilip No, Eldon, you haven't been hot yet. But you're off to the hills, so you
    will be all right.

Pike and Dilip leave

*A car is heard approaching. Flora, putting on her robe, gets out of bed and
comes to meet Durance at the steps of the verandah*

Durance enters

Flora David ... ?
Durance You're up!
Flora Up with the dawn. What on earth are you doing?
Durance (*approaching*) I'm afraid I came to wake you. Don't you sleep?
Flora Yes, I slept early and woke early.
Durance I promised you a turn with the Daimler — remember?
Flora Yes.
Durance I wanted to show you the sunrise. There's a pretty place for it only
    ten minutes down the road. Will you come?
Flora Can I go in my dressing-gown?
Durance Well ... better not.
Flora Right-o. I'll get dressed.
Durance Good.
Flora Come up.

Durance comes up the verandah steps

    I'll be quick.

She goes into the bedroom. She hurriedly puts on a dress

Durance (*calling from the verandah*) The damnedest thing happened to me
    just now.
Flora Can't hear you!

Durance steps closer, outside the bedroom door

Durance That fellow Das was on the road. I'm sure it was him.
Flora (*dressing*) Well ... why not?
Durance He cut me.
Flora What?
Durance I gave him a wave and he turned his back. I thought — "well, that's

a first!"
Flora Oh! There's hope for him yet.
Durance They'll be throwing stones next. (*Then registering her remark*) What?
Flora Come in, it's quite safe.

Durance enters the bedroom. Flora, dressed, puts on her shoes, drags a hairbrush through her hair

Durance picks up Flora's book from beside the unmade bed

Durance Oh ... ! You're reading Emily Eden. I read it years ago.
Flora We'll miss the sunrise.
Durance (*with the book*) There's a bit somewhere ... she reminds me of you. "Off with their heads!"
Flora Whose heads?
Durance Hang on, I'll find it — it was Queen Victoria's birthday ... Oh!
Flora What?
Durance Nothing. I found your bookmark.
Flora I'm ready. It's not my bookmark, I put it there for safe keeping.
Durance Where did you get such a thing?
Flora His Highness gave it to me.
Durance Why?
Flora Because I ate an apricot. Because he is a Rajah. Because he hoped I'd go to bed with him. I don't know.
Durance But how could he ... feel himself in such intimacy with you? Had you met him before?
Flora No, David ——
Durance But my dear girl, in accepting a gift like this don't you see ... (*Pause*) Well, it's your life, of course ...
Flora Shall we go?
Durance ... but I'm in a frightfully difficult position now.
Flora Why?
Durance Did he visit you?
Flora I visited him.
Durance I know. Did he visit you?
Flora Mind your own business.
Durance But it is my business.
Flora Because you think you love me?
Durance No, I ... Keeping tabs on what His Highness is up to is one of my ... I mean I write reports to Delhi.
Flora (*amused*) Oh heavens!
Durance You're a politically sensitive person, actually, coming here with an

introduction from that man Chamberlain ... I mean this sort of thing ——

Flora Oh, darling policeman.

Durance How can I ignore it?

Flora Don't ignore it. Report what you like. I don't mind, you see. You mind. But I don't. I have never minded.

Flora steps on to the verandah

(*In despair*) Oh — look at the sky! We're going to be too late!

Durance (*to hell with it*) Come on! Our road is due west — if you know how to drive a car we'll make it.

They dash towards the car ...

The car doors are heard slamming, the engine roars into life and the Daimler takes off at what sounds like a dangerous speed

Flora, with her suitcase packed, is writing at her verandah table

Flora "Oh dear, guess what? You won't approve. Quite right, darling. It's definitely time to go. Love 'em and leave 'em."

Pike enters

Pike The man was most probably the Junior Political Agent at the Residency, Captain David Arthur Durance, who took F.C. dancing and horseriding. He was killed at Kohima in March 1944 when British and Indian troops halted the advance of the Japanese forces.

Flora "I feel tons better, though. The juices are starting to flow again, see enclosed."

Pike "Pearl", included in *Indian Ink* (1932).

Flora "I'll send you fair copies of anything I finish in case I get carried away by monsoons or tigers, and if you get a pound for them put it in the Sasha fund."

Pike The reference is obscure.

Pike leaves

Mrs Swan and Anish enter. He carries his briefcase. She has Flora's copy of Emily Eden

Anish Mrs Swan ... Flora's letter said, "Guess what? You won't approve ..." ... and Mr Pike's footnote implies that it was the Political Agent, Captain

Durance, who ——
Mrs Swan Mr Pike presumes too much.
Anish Yes! Why wouldn't you approve of Captain Durance? Surely it's
more likely she meant ...
Mrs Swan Meant what, Mr Das?
Anish I don't mean any offence.
Mrs Swan Then you must take care not to give it.
Anish But would you have disapproved of a British Army Officer, Mrs
Swan? More than of an Indian painter?
Mrs Swan Certainly. Mr Pike is spot-on there. In 1930 I was working for
a communist newspaper. Which goes to show that people are surprising.
But you know that from your father, don't you?
Anish Why?
Mrs Swan He must have surprised you too. The terror of the Empire Day
gymkhana, the thrower of mangoes at the Resident's Daimler.
Anish Yes. Yes. He must have — altered.
Mrs Swan Yes. One alters.

She gives Anish the book by Emily Eden

This is yours. It belonged to your father. It has his name in it.

Anish takes the book wordlessly and opens it

I hope you're not going to blub. And you musn't make assumptions. When
Flora said I wouldn't approve, she did not mean this man or that man.
Cigarettes, whisky and men were not on the menu. She didn't need Dr
Guppy to tell her that. No, I would not have approved. But Flora's
weakness was always romance. To call it that.
Anish She had a romance with my father.
Mrs Swan Quite possibly. Or with Captain Durance. Or His Highness the
Rajah of Jummapur. Or someone else entirely. It hardly matters, looking
back. Men were not really important to Flora. If they had been, they would
have been fewer. She used them like batteries. When things went flat, she'd
put in a new one ... I'll come to the gate with you. If you decide to tell Mr
Pike about the watercolour, I'm sure Flora wouldn't mind.
Anish No. Thank you, but it's my father I'm thinking of. He really wouldn't
want it, not even in a footnote. So we'll say nothing to Mr Pike.
Mrs Swan Good for you. I don't tell Mr Pike everything either. It's been an
unusually interesting day, thanks to you, Mr Das.
Anish Thank you for tea. The Victoria sponge was best! The raspberry jam
too.
Mrs Swan I still have raspberries left to pick, and the plums to come. I always

loved the fruit trees at home.

Anish At home?

During the following, Anish leaves

Mrs Swan Orchards of apricot — almond — plum — I never cared for the southern fruits, mango, paw-paw and such like. But up in the North West ... I was quite unprepared for it when I first arrived. It was early summer. There was a wind blowing. And I have never seen such blossom, it blew everywhere. There were drifts of snow-white flowers piled up against the walls of the graveyard. I had to kneel on the ground and sweep the petals off her stone to read her name.

Mrs Swan remains

Nell is bending over a gravestone ... watched by Eric

Mrs Swan "Florence Edith Crewe ... Born March 21st 1895... Died June 10th 1930. *Requiescat In Pace.*"

Eric I'm afraid it's very simple. I hope that's all right.

Nell Yes. It was good of you.

Eric Oh no, we look after our own. Of course.

Nell I think she would have liked "Poet" under her name. If I left some money here to pay for it ... ?

Eric There are funds within my discretion. You may count on it, Miss Crewe. Poet. I should have thought of that. It is how we remember your sister.

Nell Really?

Eric She read one evening. The Club has a habit of asking guests to sing for their supper and Miss Crewe read to us ... from her work.

Nell Oh dear.

Eric (*laughing gently*) Yes. Well, we're a bit behind the times, I expect. But we all liked her very much. We didn't know what to expect because we understood she was a protegée of Mr Chamberlain who had lectured in the town some years before. Perhaps you know him.

Nell Yes. I'm not really in touch with him nowadays.

Eric Ah. It was just about this time of year when she was here, wasn't it? It was clear she wasn't well — these steps we just climbed, for instance, she could hardly manage them. Even so, death in India is often more unexpected, despite being more common, if you understand me. I'm talking far too much. I'm so sorry. I'll wait at the gate. Please stay as long as you wish, I have no-one waiting for me.

Nell I won't be a moment. Flora didn't like mopers.

Eric leaves her

(*Quietly*) Bye bye, darling ... oh—damn! (*Because she has burst into sobs. She weeps unrestrainedly*)

Eric returns

Eric Oh ... oh, I say ...
Nell Oh, I'm sorry.
Eric No — please ... can I ... ?

Nell stops crying after a few moments

Nell I've messed up your coat. I've got a hanky somewhere.
Eric Would you like to ... ? Here ...
Nell Yes. Thank you.

She uses his handkerchief

I came too soon after all. I hated waiting a whole year but ... well, anyway. Thank you, it's a bit wet. Should I keep it? Oh look, I've found mine, we can swap.
Eric Don't you worry about anything. What a shame you had to come on your own. You have another sister, I believe. Or a brother?
Nell No. Why?
Eric Oh. Flora was anxious to return to England to be an *aunt*, she said.
Nell Yes. I had a baby in October. He only lived a little while, unfortunately. There was something wrong.
Eric Oh. I'm so sorry.
Nell It's why I couldn't come before.
Eric Yes, I see. What rotten luck. What was his name?
Nell Sasha.
Mrs Swan Alexander, really. Alexander Percival Crewe.
Nell How nice of you to ask. Nobody ever does. I say, how about that blossom!
Eric Yes, it's quite a spot, isn't it? I hope you stay a while. First time in India?
Nell Yes.
Eric Mind the loose stone here. May I ... ?
Nell Thank you. I'm sorry I blubbed, Mr Swan.
Eric I won't tell anyone. Do call me Eric, by the way. Nobody calls me Mr Swan.
Nell Eric, then.
Eric Do you like cricket?
Nell (*laughing*) Well, I don't play a lot.

Eric There's a match tomorrow.
Nell Here?
Eric Oh yes. We're going to field a Test team next year, you know.
Nell We?
Eric India.
Nell Oh.

As they go, Pike enters, looking for the right grave. He finds it, he takes his hat off and stands looking at it

During the following, Nell enters

Flora "Darling, that's all from Jummapur, because now I'm packed, portrait and all, and Mr Coomaraswami is coming to take me to the station. I'll post this in Jaipur as soon as I get there. I'm not going to post it here because I'm not. I feel fit as two lops this morning, and happy, too, because something good happened here which made me feel halfway better about Modi and getting back to Paris too late. That was a sin I'll carry to my grave, but perhaps my soul will stay behind as a smudge of paint on paper, as if I'd always been here, like Radha who was the most beautiful of the herdswomen, undressed for love in an empty house."

Flora puts her letter into an envelope and seals it

Elsewhere, Nell kneels on the floor, going through the contents of Flora's — duplicate — suitcase. She looks at the blue dress briefly. She finds the rolled-up canvas. She looks at it and puts it back

Nazrul enters to take Flora's suitcase to the train

Flora goes to the train carrying her copy of Emily Eden

The train makes its reappearance. Coomaraswami, holding his yellow parasol, is on the station platform to take leave of Flora. He garlands her. Nazrul puts Flora's suitcase on the rack above her seat. Flora enters the train compartment, gives Nazrul a tip, and bids him farewell

Nell finds Flora's copy of the Emily Eden book in the suitcase. She opens it and finds the Rajah's gift in the book. She replaces the "bookmark" and glances through the book

Flora waves as the train starts to depart. During the recording of Emily Eden's letter, Flora finds her place in the book, and is reading it to herself as we hear her voice

Flora (*recorded*) "Simla, Saturday, May 25th, 1839. The Queen's Ball 'came off' yesterday with great success ... Between the two tents there was a boarded platform for dancing, roped and arched in with flowers ... There was a very old Hindu temple also prettily lit up. Vishnu, to whom I believe it really belonged, must have been affronted. It was the most beautiful evening; such a moon, and the mountains looked so soft and grave, after all the fireworks and glare. Twenty years ago no European had ever been here, and there we were with a band playing, and observing that St Cloup's Potage à la Julienne was perhaps better than his other soups, and so on, and all this in the face of those high hills, and we one hundred and five Europeans being surrounded by at least three thousand Indians, who looked on at what we call our polite amusements, and bowed to the ground if a European came near them. I sometimes wonder they do not cut all our heads off and say nothing more about it.'

The train clatters loudly and fades with the light

CURTAIN

FURNITURE AND PROPERTY LIST

ACT I

On stage: Railway compartment seat with luggage rack above. *On rack*: **Flora**'s suitcase

Microphone (optional)

GUESTHOUSE VERANDAH
Small table. *On it*: notebook, fountain pen
Wicker chairs

GUESTHOUSE BEDROOM
Bed with mosquito net. *On it*: sheets, pillows
Bedside table. *On it*: glass with beaded lace cover
Washstand. *On it*: jug of water
Electric ceiling fan
"Punkah"

SHEPPERTON GARDEN
Two garden chairs
Garden table. *On it*: shoebox containing letters, tray containing two cups and saucers, teapot, sugar bowl, milk jug, plates, madeira cake, second cake, knife

Off stage: Garland (**Coomaraswami**)
Tray of drinks (**Servant**)
Canvas, bicycle with wooden work box attached containing artist's materials, cloth, and an old, well-preserved copy of Emily Eden's *Up the Country* (**Das**)
Soft briefcase containing hardback copy of "The Collected Letters of Flora Crewe" with dustjacket, artist's block, pencil, watercolour between two stiff boards (**Anish Das**)
Tray with two cups and saucer, spoons, milk jug, pot of tea, plates, two kinds of cake (**Mrs Swan**)
Tray containing jug of lemonade and two glasses (**Nazrul**)
Tea-tray with tea for two (**Nazrul**)
Bottle of cola, bag containing "The Collected Letters of Flora Crewe" (**Dilip**)
White towel (**Das**)
Canvas portrait of Flora rolled inside a cardboard tube (**Mrs Swan**)

Shopping (**Nazrul**)
Bottle of soda water (**Das**)

Personal: **Coomaraswami**: yellow parasol
Mrs Swan: handkerchief
Das: small sketchpad, fountain pen, folding easel, cigarettes, box of
    matches
Pike: smart shoulder bag containing a camera

ACT II

On stage: JUMMAPUR CLUB VERANDAH
Tables
Chairs
Two gymnasium horses. *On them*: stirrups, reins. *On one*: solar topee
Two polo sticks
Topee
Other various items

GARDEN/COURTYARD OF JUMMAPUR PALACE HOTEL
Tables
Chairs

SHEPPERTON GARDEN
Table. *On it*: two glasses of gin-and-tonic, watercolour, miniature
    watercolour
Two chairs

GUESTHOUSE VERANDAH
Small table. *On it*: notepaper, envelope, fountain pen, copy of Emily
    Eden's *Up the Country*
Wicker chairs

GUESTHOUSE BEDROOM
Bed with mosquito net. *On it*: sheets, pillows, robe
Bedside table. *On it*: glass with beaded lace cover, hairbrush, book
Washstand. *On it*: jug of water
Electric ceiling fan
"Punkah"

Off stage: Faded beige gabardine jacket and striped tie (**Dilip**)
Two tumblers of whisky and a soda syphon on a salver (**Servant**)
Two American colas (**Waiter**)
Note (**Waiter**)
Tray of drinks, fruit (tangerines, bananas, lychees, apricots, etc.),
    cigarette box, finger bowls, napkins (**Servant**)

Bottle of beer (**Dilip**)
Bottle of beer (**Pike**)
Flora's suitcase (**Stage Management**)
Flora's copy of Emily Eden's *Up the Country* (**Mrs Swan**)
Gravestone (**Stage Management**)
Duplicate of **Flora**'s suitcase containing **Flora**'s blue dress, rolled-up
    canvas and copy of *Up the Country* with miniature watercolour
    "bookmark" (**Stage Management**)
Railway compartment seat with luggage rack above (**Stage Manage-
    ment**)
Garland (**Coomaraswami**)

Personal: **Rajah**: letter, copy of letter
           Anish: wallet containing newspaper clipping
           Das: small paper-wrapped watercolour in pocket
           Eric: handkerchief

LIGHTING PLOT

Practical fittings required: electric light in guesthouse, oil lamp on verandah

Various interior and exterior settings

ACT I

To open: Lighting on train compartment area

Cue 1	As **Flora** speaks *Bring up lighting for railway station*	(Page 1)
Cue 2	**Flora**: "Are you Mr Coomar ..." *Bring up daylight effect on guesthouse verandah with dim interior in bedroom*	(Page 1)
Cue 3	**Coomaraswami** leaves **Flora** *Bring up lighting on Shepperton garden*	(Page 2)
Cue 4	**Pike**: "May I?" *Bring up daylight effect on sightseeing area*	(Page 4)
Cue 5	**Flora**: "My lecture drew a packed house ..." *Dim lighting on guesthouse and cross-fade from sightseeing area to night exterior effect on courtyard area*	(Page 5)
Cue 6	**Flora, Coomaraswami** and **Das** go *Fade night exterior effect on courtyard area*	(Page 7)
Cue 7	**Mrs Swan**: "... sixty years ago?" *Bring up sunlight on verandah with dim lighting on guesthouse interior*	(Page 8)
Cue 8	**Mrs Swan** leaves *Fade lighting on Shepperton Garden*	(Page 23)
Cue 9	**Flora**: "Oh, Mr Das!" *Bring up lighting on modern Indian street area*	(Page 27)
Cue 10	**Pike** follows **Dilip** off *Fade lighting on modern Indian street area*	(Page 30)

Cue 11	**Das** disappears round the corner	(Page 35)
	Bring up lighting on Shepperton garden area	

ACT II

To open: Evening light on Jummapur Club area and verandah

Cue 12	**Durance**: "I'll show you."	(Page 48)
	Cross-fade to exterior effect	

Cue 13	The horses trot	(Page 50)
	Cross-fade to sunlight effect on hotel garden/courtyard area	

Cue 14	**Pike** goes	(Page 57)
	Cross-fade to exterior effect on Shepperton garden	

Cue 15	**Pike**: "... of the army in Afghanistan.'	(Page 59)
	Cross-fade to night effect on guesthouse verandah; as scene progresses bring up moonlight effect	

Cue 16	Car is heard	(Page 59)
	Sweep of car headlights	

Cue 17	**Coomaraswami** lights the oil lamp	(Page 60)
	Bring up oil lamp practical with covering spot	

Cue 18	**Das** switches on the electric light	(Page 62)
	Snap on practical in guesthouse with covering spot	

Cue 19	**Flora** turns down the oil lamp	(Page 62)
	Reduce oil lamp practical and covering spot	

Cue 20	**Flora**: "It doesn't matter."	(Page 63)
	Snap off all practicals and covering spots	

Cue 21	They stand still	(Page 64)
	Moonlight clouds to darkness; when ready bring up dawn effect on guesthouse and verandah, gradually increasing as scene progresses	

Cue 22	Daimler roars off at high speed	(Page 68)
	Change to daylight effect on guesthouse verandah with dim light in bedroom	

Cue 23	**Pike** leaves	(Page 68)
	Bring up exterior effect on Shepperton garden	

EFFECTS PLOT

Act I

ACT II

Cue 13   To open   (Page 41)
            Gramophone music

Cue 14   **Englishman**: "The collectingness is terrific."   (Page 42)
            Another record begins to play

Cue 15   **Dilip** enters   (Page 42)
            Fade music

Cue 16   **Pike**: "He must be pretty ancient."   (Page 44)
            Gramophone music fades in

Cue 17   The **Servant** bows and leaves   (Page 45)
            Fade music

Cue 18   **Durance**: "I'll show you."   (Page 48)
            Horses whinny

Cue 19   The scene becomes exterior   (Page 48)
            *Ground mist; horses whinny and sound of cantering; birds
               crying out, distancing rapidly*

Cue 20   **Flora**: " ... stop!"   (Page 48)
            Horses halt

Cue 21   **Flora**: "'Fraid so." She laughs   (Page 49)
            Horses trot; fading away

Cue 22   **Rajah**: "... and they did the sitting."   (Page 52)
            Sound of cars passing by slowly one by one; continue

Cue 23   **Rajah**: "... you won't win by playing cricket."   (Page 53)
            Sound of cars stops

Cue 24   **Flora**: "... I'm going to leave it to you."   (Page 54)
            Car purrs by in front

Cue 25   **Flora**: "Then I accept."   (Page 54)
            Another car goes by; sound of musical car horn

Cue 26   The **Rajah** signals for the car to stop   (Page 55)
            Sound of car stops idling

Cue 27   **Flora** leaves the stage   (Page 55)
            Cut sound of idling car

Cue 28	**Nirad Das** and **Coomaraswami** sit on the verandah *Sound car pulling up and then driving away*	(Page 59)
Cue 29	**Coomaraswami** shouts towards somebody distant *Approaching jingle of harness, horse and buggy*	(Page 61)
Cue 30	**Flora**: "He is leaving you behind." *Sound of horse and buggy departing*	(Page 62)
Cue 31	The moonlight clouds to darkness **Flora**'s recorded voice as script page 64	(Page 64)
Cue 32	**Pike** and **Dilip** leave *Sound of a car approaching and stopping*	(Page 66)
Cue 33	They dash towards the car *Car doors slam, engine starts and roars off at high speed*	(Page 68)
Cue 34	**Flora** waves *Sound of train pulling out of the station;* **Flora**'s recorded *voice as script page 73; train clatters loudly*	(Page 72)
Cue 35	The Lights begin to fade *Fade train sound in sequence with lighting*	(Page 73)